9.80

The International Book of
BEER LABELS

Keith Osborne

MATS & COASTERS

Brian Pipe

CHARTWELL BOOKS INC.

Opposite half-title
The very dated-looking
Booths Gin series, and six of
the 'Baby Bubbly' girls.

Half-title
Lovely ladies from all over
the world undoubtedly
sharpen the interest of the
male beer drinker and
labologist alike.

Title spread
Top row, from left to right:
a replica of a Bass water jug;
a bottle of English Guinness
Silver Jubilee Ale; a bottle of
Courage Star Bicentennial
Ale; a bottle of Bass Ratcliff
Ale dated 16/12/1869; a
bottle of Bass Kings Ale
dated 22/2/1902; an
original Hoare and Company
Toby Jug; a bottle of
Eldridge Pope's numbered
Thomas Hardy's Ale. Centre,
from left to right: Bernards
90/- Pale Ale; a John
Roberts 'home brew' mat
issued by CAMRA; a Barclay
Perkins 1953 Coronation mat;
and a bottle of Gales 'Corked'
Prize Old Ale. Bottom row,
from left to right: a Fullers
towel mat; a Bernards 1955
mat; a Starkey Knight &
Fords mat, c. 1956; a Taylor
Walkers 1951 Festival of
Britain mat; a Bass 1963
Export mat with a diamond
trade mark; and a Greene
King ash tray.

Title verso
Beer mats can be many
different shapes. Included
here are an Ind Coope
Trident design mat, a
Drybrough's rosette mat and
an Everard's Tiger mat
(which can be found with
both black and orange
wording on the reverse).

Contents page
A Brew for All Seasons:
Easter or Spring ales are
popular in Scandinavia and
Germany and the occasional
Pinse Bryg (Whitsuntide
brew) appears in Denmark.
Summer, Autumn and
Winter are represented too in
this group of labels for
seasonal brews.

790.13
OSB

Published by The Hamlyn Publishing Group Limited 1979
Astronaut House, Feltham, Middlesex, England

This edition published by Chartwell Books Inc.,
A division of Book Sales Inc.,
110 Enterprise Avenue, Secaucus, New Jersey 07094

© Copyright The Hamlyn Publishing Group Limited 1979

ISBN 0-89009-253-2
LOC Catalog Card Number 78-68035

Filmset by Tradespools Ltd., Frome, Somerset, England
Printed in Hong Kong by Leefung-Asco Printers Ltd.

Contents

Introduction

I must confess that I don't collect beer labels. When I have tried to steam labels off bottles, the wretched things have always torn and I have scalded my fingers. (This book suggests a simpler method that hadn't occurred to me: write to the brewery companies and ask for some labels that aren't attached to bottles.)

My tiny collection of beer mats is used exclusively to protect my office desk from hot cups of tea, something that in tegestological circles will be considered akin to *lèse majesté*. But we are kindred spirits, these avid collectors and I, for we all delight in the simple pleasures of beer.

Wine is for connoisseurs but beer is for fun. Beer is warm memories of foaming glasses in cheerful pubs, inns and bars. If you think back to some of the best moments of your life, beer is likely to figure in them somewhere.

I suspect that this is why the craze for label and mat collecting really began, as a way of recalling those special occasions when the beer flowed, the company was good and the conversation sparkled. Browsing through old labels and mats is a merry trip down memory lane.

But now, as this fascinating book shows, collecting has become almost a way of life for those who have really caught the bug. There are clubs, societies, conferences and magazines all over the world, and collaboration and swapping takes place on an international scale.

Labels and mats are small but important social documents, for they trace the rise of the brewing industries in many countries and follow the success of some companies and the demise of many more. They follow, too, the changing tastes of beer drinkers, such as the nineteenth-century popularity of darker beers and the modern trend towards lighter-coloured lagers and bitters.

Labels and mats are cheap and simple methods of advertising. The clear designs, bright colours and catchy slogans are devised to stimulate awareness of the products as well as the drinkers' taste buds. But slogans can rebound on the brewers: when the British producers of Double Diamond promoted the beer on mats with such one-liners as 'DD4U', some drinkers responded with badges declaring 'DD is K9P'.

Labels and mats can be informative. A delicious strong ale, Worthington White Shield, brewed by Bass in Burton-on-Trent in England, has a series of notches on the bottle labels that form a brewer's code to identify the week, the month and the quarter of the year in which each batch was brewed. As this beer has the yeasty sediment left in the bottles, once you have cracked the code you will know when the beer is in peak condition for drinking. This same beer generated one of the most bizarre examples of brewers' advertising – a 1930s Daimler motor car designed in the shape of a giant bottle of beer. It can still be seen and driven in the Bass museum at Burton.

A splendid series of award-winning beer mats that humorously traces the history of beer and brewing was produced in 1976 by another Burton company, Ind Coope. The mats celebrated the production of a new draught beer called Burton Ale and they will command a special place in the collections of British tegestologists, for the beer marked an amazing about-turn in brewing history. For several decades the major brewers had dominated the market with sterile keg beers but a consumer revolt led by the Campaign for Real Ale prompted Ind Coope and several other companies to start brewing living, traditional and tasty draught beer on a major scale again. The Burton Ale mats, with their Mickey Mouse ears, are proof that brewers ignore the consumers at their peril.

The authors record the sad decline in the number of brewing companies in most countries in the twentieth century. While Germany and Belgium have escaped major takeovers and mergers and retain hundreds of small regional breweries, brewing in the United States, Britain and France is dominated by giant companies, which is bad news for collectors and often for drinkers. But now the tide is beginning to flow in the other direction: new small breweries are springing up throughout the British Isles – there were 20 of them in 1978 – and a few similar operations have started successfully on the West Coast of the United States.

More choice means more labels, more beer mats and more pleasure. Beer is alive and well in bottle and cask and this book is testimony to that happy fact.

ROGER PROTZ
Editor, *The Good Beer Guide*

Opposite
Christmas: the season of goodwill and celebration all over the world. The Christmas spirit is captured completely in this display of labels advertising strong ales brewed for the occasion in Norway, England, Denmark, Germany, Canada, Sweden, Belgium, the United States, Austria and Finland.

BEER LABELS

The collecting craze

Why collect beer labels? True, they are small and colourful, but then so are many other collectable objects such as matchbox labels, cheese labels, cigarette cards, bus tickets and railway tickets, none of which appear on the surface to have much value. Yet while most people are familiar with philately, have perhaps come across philumeny (match-box label collecting), and are even aware of cartopholy (cigarette card collecting), they are probably unlikely to have heard of labology – the official term for beer label collecting.

Yet there are countless reasons for collecting beer labels. They range from the beer drinker wishing to have a record of the brews he has tried, to the social historian using the beer label to illustrate changing public tastes in beer. Nostalgia plays its part too: many a time an old label will bring a twinkle to the eye of an old gentleman who recalls the ale he used to enjoy in his youth. Countless mergers and takeovers have meant that a few large companies now dominate the beer world, and the brewery he remembers probably no longer exists. It is this that gives another interest to label collecting.

The disappearance of so many of the world's breweries over the last 100 years has meant that there are many obsolete labels to collect. In the United Kingdom alone, there were over 6,000 'brewers for sale' in 1900; by 1939, the number had dropped to 1,418 and in 1979 there are only 170. One American city, Philadelphia, had 94 breweries in 1879; a century later, it has two. The scope for collecting is vast, therefore, and to obtain a label which dates from the last century is a feat in itself. Most dedicated collectors are more enthusiastic about obsolete labels than about current ones, although fascination with the latter will doubtless grow as the years pass. Beer labels, then, are certainly more than colourful pieces of paper: they are historical records of the world's breweries and the beers which they have produced.

But that is not the only fascination of beer labels. The hobby is extensive by nature: the number and variety of labels which have been issued is infinite, giving the enthusiast many opportunities to expand his collection and keeping his interest active. Many collectors also specialize in brewery history, for knowledge of the development and demise of a brewery makes them appreciate the rarity of its advertising material. And some labels have a whole story to tell. The bear gates on the label issued by the Traquair House brewery near Innerleithen in Scotland, for example, have been kept securely locked and bolted since Bonnie Prince Charlie sheltered there in 1745. The Jubilee label issued by the Faxe brewery in Denmark in 1956 records the hundred and fiftieth anniversary of the postal service, while the Carbine Stout label of Castlemaine Perkins, Brisbane, depicts probably the most famous racehorse ever to run on Australian turf.

Beer label collecting as an organized hobby is only about 20 years old, and most labologist societies and associations have sprung up since 1958. However, there were notable collectors well before that time. The late Norton Price of Margate, England began collecting in 1911 when, as a boy in his father's off-licence, he soaked the labels from the various empty bottles which were returned. Today these labels are unique. In the late 1950s his enthusiasm was really fired, and by his death in 1971, he had managed to amass over 16,000 British beer labels, as well as a first class collection of labels from breweries in the United States. Had he spent his life collecting seriously, there is no doubt that he would have accumulated the most comprehensive collection in the world.

The United States has produced some notable collectors. In 1963, P. A. Miller of Milwaukee was reported to have 125,000 different beer labels from all over the world, while his fellow Americans Walter Ronda and H. N. Mick had 45,000 and 22,000 respectively. Some collectors in Europe, particularly Eastern Europe, have probably amassed as many, if not more: Werner Zimmerman of East Germany was known to have collected more than 100,000 labels in 1965, while Anton Thürner of Worgl, Austria possibly had an even larger collection.

Today the most famous American collector is without doubt 'Uncle' Ernie Oest of Port Jefferson Station, New York, who has gathered together, since the 1920s, over 125,000 beer labels from all parts of the world, with over 21,000 from the

Five labels with stories behind them. Carbine, the celebrated Australian racehorse, appears on the Castlemaine Perkins label; the rising smoke on the Hokonui Draught label tells of the illicit whisky stills which could once be found in this part of New Zealand; the hundred and fiftieth anniversary of the Danish Postal Service is commemorated by the label from the Faxe Brewery; and the back label for the Traquair House Ale bottle explains the secret of the bear gates at this ancient Scottish stately home.

Unique labels from the Canterbury Brewery Company, England, soaked from their bottles in 1912 by the late Norton Price, and now in the author's collection.

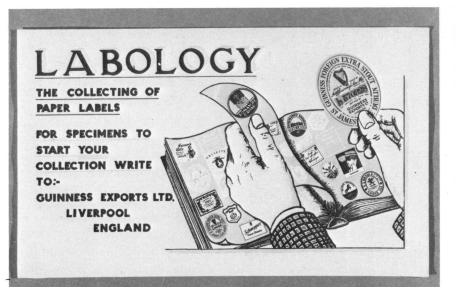

United States alone. Ernie Oest's interest in beer labels stems from the days of Prohibition, when he first encountered the different brands of 'near beer' which was the only beer available at the time. Beer labels comprise only a part of his vast collection of brewery advertising items which was at one time on display to the public in a museum at his home.

In the United Kingdom, a most remarkable collection of some 100,000 examples from non-British breweries all over the world, is held by Miss Joan Connew at her home in Bromley, Kent. The largest collection of British beer labels is held by the author. Although large, totalling more than 22,000, the collection probably represents less than a third of the breweries which have operated in the United Kingdom since the turn of the century.

There is no doubt that greater organization of the hobby has meant that collectors have been able to discover new and hitherto unexplored

avenues, and this has helped in the building up of larger collections. The oldest organization for the beer label collector is the Labologists Society of England, which is international in character, despite the predominant British element, and small membership (about 250 at present). The Society was founded in September 1958 as a result of an idea by Peter Dawson to unite the beer label collectors of the world. With the help of the late Harold Hordern, and assistance from Colonel William Fawcett acting on behalf of Guinness Exports Ltd. the hobby was publicized widely and an office was found in London. Interest by the company, which had seen the hobby as a good public relations venture, later waned and the present independent society was subsequently formed. An illustrated newsletter is issued every two months containing, among other things, articles on brewery history, developments in the brewing industries of the various countries, information on new label issues, features on obsolete labels, information on beer generally and a members' advertising service.

Organized beer label collecting has also spread to many other parts of the world. In the early 1970s, the Australian Labologists Club was founded by F. Simpson of Toowoomba, Queensland and in 1972, chiefly through the efforts of Phil Davin and John Long, a small number of enthusiasts from Melbourne came together to establish the Victorian Beer Label Collectors Society. The latter produces a high-quality twelve-page illustrated newsletter every two months, and has provided its members with Special Anniversary beers, complete with appropriately designed labels. Australia's other beer label collecting organization–the Adelaide Labology Group–was formed in July 1974 and produces a monthly newsletter comprising a single sheet. New Zealand, which previously had *The Labologist Review*, now has, thanks to Brian Ronson, *The New Zealand Beer Label Collectors'*

Magazine, established in 1977 and published monthly.

Scandinavian collectors also have their own magazine, *Samlerringen*, from Copenhagen, now in its eleventh year of publication, as the organ of the *Skandaninavisk Bryggerisouvenir Samlerforening*. Elsewhere in Europe, there are publications of interest to label collectors but which also cater for collectors of a whole range of brewery artifacts. *Unser Steckenpferd* ('Our Hobby'), established in 1959, covers West Germany, Switzerland and Austria. Both *Unser Steckenpferd* and *Bierdeckel Magazin*–founded in 1962 and with over 600 members from 27 countries–cover beer mat collecting, but include 'etiketten' or labels, the latter specializing more in 'breweriana'.

In the United States, the oldest brewery souvenir organization is the 'Eastern Coast Breweriana Association' with some 400 members who collect all kinds of brewery relics, including beer labels. The Association was founded in 1970 in Hicksville, New York and issues a quarterly newsletter. The addresses of all these societies can be found in an appendix at the back of the book. The existence of these organizations, and many other informal labologist groups in various countries, proves the growing popularity of beer label collecting. Probably the Eastern European countries, especially Czechoslovakia–which has a rich brewing tradition–have the largest number of beer label collectors, and an international exchange meeting for brewery artifacts of all kinds is held annually in Czechoslovakia.

Beer label collecting is a hobby on a truly international scale. The albums of labologists across the globe provide a fascinating and colourful insight into the beers and breweries of the world, both past and present. Takeovers, mergers and closures of breweries may have removed many of the popular brands from the inns and taverns but at least they are not forgotten.

History of the beer label

Opposite
Auxiliary labels of different shapes and styles from Germany and Britain. They appear on the neck or stopper of the bottle, and in some cases, are the only label used.

The East India Pale Ale tradition: the earliest known label, dated 1843 from Bass of Burton-on-Trent, England, (shown at the bottom of the photograph), is dwarfed by 20th-century cask and bottle labels advertising the same brew.

Bottled products bore paper labels in the seventeenth century. Early drug phials had a label which covered the whole of the glass and early in the following century, patent medicine vendors were using paper labels widely. The first use of labels on alcohol bottles seems to have come in the middle of the eighteenth century: it is known, for example, that a black and white label was being used for port wine in 1756. Up to the 1860s, bottles of wine were sold in cases largely to members of the upper and middle classes, and were therefore not distributed widely; around that time, however, concern that a wider public should have access to wine (partly to counteract the widescale consumption of spirits) gave rise to legislation to allow any retailer to sell wine in single bottles, and each bottle had to have a label.

Beer labels were probably unknown before the 1840s. In England, beer was not bottled to any great extent until 1834, when the duty on glass was repealed. Before that time, the customer had his own bottles which were impressed with his own seal – usually showing a coat of arms or name, together with the date – just below the neck of the bottle. After 1834, bottles were still sealed by hand. The name of the brewer and a description of the contents was stamped into the neck of the wax seal. Because of expanding trade, a quicker method of identification was developed: a metal foil capsule, similar to those still used today for the bottling of wines and spirits, was soon introduced. This depicted the brewer's name and nature of contents. There was, however, a disadvantage in that when the bottle was handled roughly the cap soon became illegible. Printed paper labels were therefore the answer.

The growth of cities caused by the Industrial Revolution in England enabled brewers to 'mass produce' their beer, while in rural districts, the decline of home brewing increased the sales of country brewers. Population increases in American cities, largely through immigration, also led to brewing on a large scale, although it was predominantly national in character. Anheuser-Busch, the largest brewery company in the world, was founded in St. Louis by a German immigrant in 1852 and was the first to market beer right across the United States.

With beer being sold on an increasingly wide scale, brewers recognized the importance of identifying their products properly, and for this the label was vital. One result of British settlement in India was the export of light ale specially brewed for the climate, appropriately named 'East India Pale Ale'. Because bottled beer has a longer life than casked beer, it was more extensively used for this brew, which is invariably found advertised on the earliest labels. Labelled bottles were probably in general use in the United Kingdom by 1855, due to the extensions of the railways and canals which allowed the brewers to expand their markets. During the Crimean War, they were being exported in quantity. (A bottle with a faded label from that period is kept at William Younger's Brewery in Edinburgh.)

Owing to changing methods of sealing bottles, a new type of label came to be used: the stopper label. As the yeast in beer naturally builds up large quantities of CO_2, the cork was usually sealed with wax or foil cap and wire to prevent the force of the gas driving the cork out, particularly with export ales. In 1872, the screw stopper was patented by Henry Barrett of England and began to replace the cork, although corks were still in general use in England in the 1930s, while in Ireland they lasted to 1970. (In Belgium,

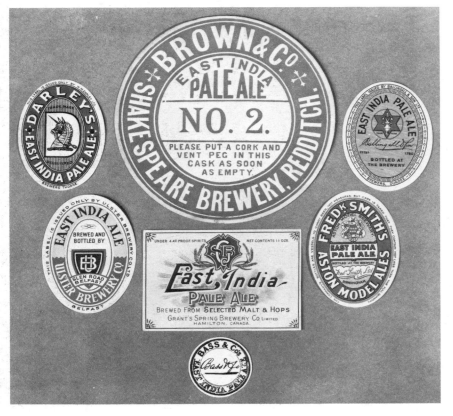

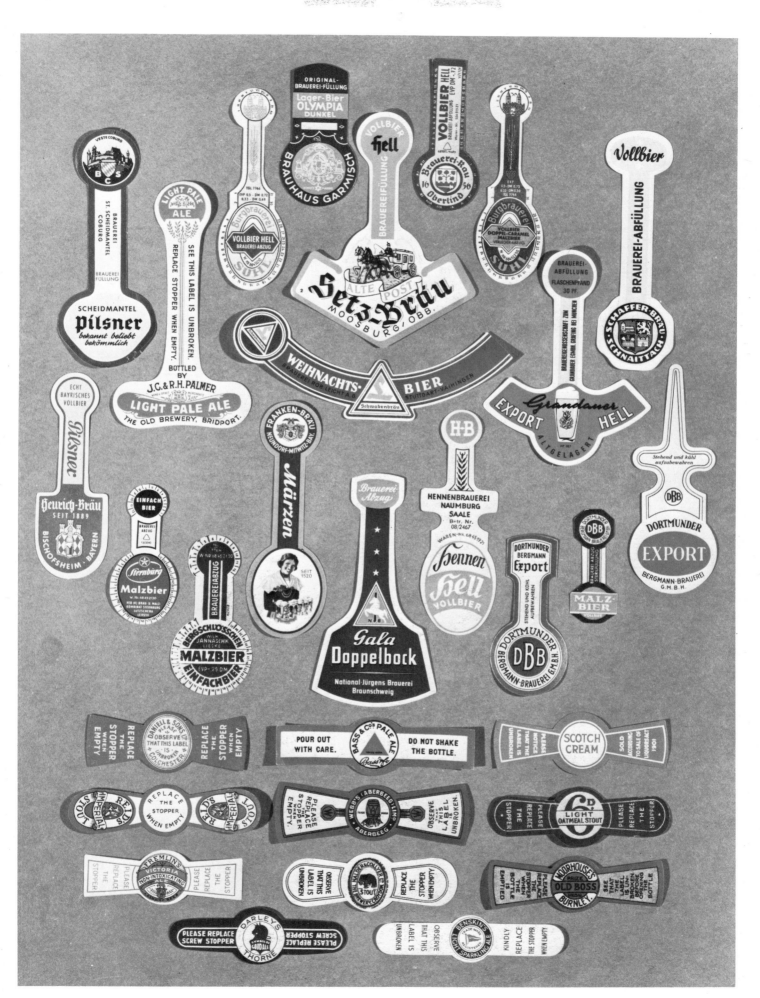

17

Late 19th-century English labels bearing the names of Scottish and European bottlers.

A selection of labels from the album of infringements and forgeries held at Bass's Brewery, Burton-on-Trent. On each label is either a device which can be confused with Bass's triangular trade mark (top row) or the protectionist background peculiar to Bass.

Opposite
Three groups of labels which illustrate three different principles of beer label design. On the top, those from the Fredrikstad Bryggeri in Norway show the tendency of some breweries to adopt a common shape and design for all their labels, merely varying the colours for the different brews. In the centre, a most striking ultra-modern design dominates the labels of the Lillehammer Bryggeri, another Norwegian company, while the labels on the bottom show that the use of one or two colours, combined with a bold, simple design, can be very effective.

Liefmans Brewery of Ouedenaarde still uses corked litres and jeroboams for its beers, and Gales of Horndean, England, have corked bottles for their Prize Old Ale. Hardy Ale, when it was introduced by Eldridge Pope, of Dorchester, England in 1968, appeared in similar bottles.)

In 1892 crown corks (metal closures with a corrugated edge which fit on the lip of the bottle and which can be levered off with a bottle opener but not satisfactorily replaced) were invented by William Painter, and they further reduced the use of ordinary corks. When screw stoppers were brought into general use, top straps to cover them soon followed. In 1901 in England, the passing of the Intoxicating Liquors (Sale to Children) Act made it necessary for all bottles that could easily be opened to bear such a strap label, some straps even mentioning the Act. In England, the stopper label is now largely a thing of the past, owing to the increased use of the crown cork on pints and quarts. Because of the small size of the stopper label, its design shows more ingenuity and taste

than that of the larger 'side' label, and this is the reason why stopper labels can add a final touch to any collection.

Perhaps the most fascinating aspect of stopper labels is the wide variety of inscriptions. The most common is 'Observe (or see) that this label is unbroken'. This is varied occasionally with 'This label should be unbroken when received', and sometimes the word 'unbroken' is replaced by 'intact' or 'entire', another slight variation being the substitution of 'capsule' or 'seal' for 'label'. In a slightly different vein is the delightful 'This label must be entire when bottle is handed to messenger'. Another common inscription to be found on the stopper label is 'Replace the stopper when empty'. Some brewers were more polite, however, adding the word 'please' or 'kindly' to the request, while others were more direct, giving the order 'screw stopper tightly'. Advice to the drinker is frequent, with 'pour out with care', 'do not shake the bottle' and 'none genuine without this label'. At times, the price of beer appears.

The world's breweries have released labels of all shapes and sizes. The conventional oval—the most common of all designs—is best illustrated by the label from the North Somerset Brewery in England (extreme left, fourth line from top).

21

A selection of European labels issued during the Second World War. The paper shortage meant that labels were often smaller in size.

The name of the brewer or brand of the beer is occasionally seen on the tab, but this is mostly reserved for the centre of the label which fits over the stopper itself.

Of equal fascination to the collector is a similar type of label used in Germany, Holland and other European countries. This fits vertically on the neck of the bottle and is sometimes the only label used. Grölsch of Holland use bottles with porcelain 'swing' top closures (devices for removing the cork or stopper by pressing two wire bales which pass through the stopper and lock against the neck of the bottle) for some of their beers, and the raised lettering on the bottles themselves necessitates a label on the neck rather than the main part of the bottle.

In the early days of bottled beer, the majority of brewers in Great Britain and Ireland left the bottling to individual shops, public houses and wholesalers. Most brewers established their own bottling stores in the early twentieth century, but Whitbread of London founded theirs in 1868. The early labels of the London breweries Barclay Perkins and Combe & Company and Guinness in Dublin bear names of different bottlers, and a selection of Guinness labels issued by various bottlers can be seen at the company's museum at the St. James's Gate Brewery, Dublin.

Trade expansion led to an increase in competition among brewers, and inevitably, undesirable practices crept in. Imitations of the best ales were sold; for example, Scotch ale by an American company was sold as Scotch in the United States. And before legislation was introduced from 1875 onwards governing trade marks, other companies could copy these without the established or authentic users having the full protection of the law. Guinness, William Younger and especially Bass suffered from this practice and an

album of some 1,900 forgeries and copyright infringements is still retained at Bass's brewery at Burton-on-Trent.

The Bass red triangle, as depicted on the Pale Ale label, is perhaps the world's best known trade mark. The story is that a loyal employee sat on the steps of the registrar's office all night to ensure that the red triangle was the first trade mark to be registered in 1890 under the Trade Marks Acts; Bass's diamond trade mark was the second entry. Both marks had, however, already been used for many years. The Bass label has a further claim to fame: it is shown on a bottle in Edouard Manet's famous painting of 1882, 'Le Bar aux Folies Bergères'.

The decade 1880–90 saw great expansion of bottled beer production due to the introduction of machinery for that purpose. This is borne out by the fact that about one third of all breweries in the United Kingdom date their first labels from that period. Owing to the amalgamation of many breweries after the First World War, and loss of overseas markets, there was a considerable decrease in the number and variety of the labels used.

Just before the Second World War, bottles with permanent fired-on or stencilled labels were introduced in England. While they were of some use during the wartime paper shortage, they were not popular, because of the time that had to be spent in sorting at the bottle store. Brewers which made use of the fired-on label included Bullard's, Steward & Patteson and Morgan's of Norwich and Campbell Praed of Wellingborough. They are still used for the bottled abbey brews of Chimay in Belgium.

The paper shortage in the Second World War also meant that some brewers, especially in the United Kingdom, stopped issuing labels and instead designated the type of beer, in small bottles, by the colour of the crown cork. Others, such as the Sønderby Bryggeri in Denmark, McLennan & Urquhart of Scotland and Trumans of England reduced the size of their labels. One English brewery – Ind Coope & Allsopp – even went as far as to specify the reason for the change: 'Miniature label necessitated by War Conditions'.

The beer label today is still essentially a means of advertising. To promote the product, and to attract the required custom on the bar shelf, a good label must be simple and bold in its design. The manufacture of special beers tends to give rise to special labels, and foil has been used in a number of countries, especially the United States and Canada. British labels have in the past tended to be rather conservative. Unlike many labels from other parts of the world, they are not pictorial, but generally depict the brewer's name, trade mark or motif and brand name, although the introduction of regulations affecting contents and the country of origin has, in the opinion of some, devalued the design to a certain extent, as the additional wording tends to clutter up the label. D. H. Tew, in an article entitled 'A Critical Study of Beer Labels', written in 1948, described beer label design as falling into two main categories. Some brewers, such as Schous of Norway, use a standard design and stick to it for all their products, while others use different designs and even different shapes for each brand. The former practice makes the public familiar with the label and the latter enables the customer to recognize what they want at a glance.

Many brewers have continued the original designs of their grandfather's day, possibly to appease their customers who might find it difficult to recognize the product in a new package; others may be reluctant to change because of the tradition associated with the beer. Some British brewers, notably Brakspears of Henley-on-Thames and the Donnington Brewery, have actually returned to the old design after using labels in a more modern style. And Australian drinkers caused such an uproar when Carlton & United Breweries removed Ballarat Bertie from the Ballarat Bitter label in 1972 that he was re-introduced within two months. One of the most famous British designs which changed little between 1907 and 1965 was the head of a cape buffalo, depicted on the Rustic Ale originally brewed by Brandon's Putney Brewery, and later continued by Mann, Crossman & Paulin Ltd. and subsequently Watney Mann.

The cape buffalo design was popular partly because it lent itself to the circular label – the earliest beer label shape. Bass of Burton-on-Trent were, by 1843, using a small circular printed label similar to the wax seal and fastened to the bottle in the same position. Labels grew in size from then on, and became more colourful, particularly when used for export, although small circular labels similar to the Bass labels, which were printed black and white, were in use for Guinness Stout up to the 1930s.

After the circle the next shape to evolve was the oval, probably the most common beer label shape. The conventional design of the oval label consists of a part cut out in the middle in the shape of an 'o', with a band stretched (either horizontally or diagonally) across it. On the band is the brand name and the name and address of the brewer appears in the top and bottom parts of the label respectively. The use of rectangular labels has increased in recent years owing to the intro-duction of high speed labelling machines. Rec-tangular labels have always been more common in North America, although the transition from oval to rectangular in other countries has been gradual, and has often been effected by combining the basic oval shape with a black rectangular background.

Over the years, there has been much variation in the basic shapes of labels, of which there are 15: circular, oval, pear-shaped, rectangular, square, shield, barrel, triangular, diamond, oc-tagonal, hexagonal, parallelogram, saddle, cres-cent and loaf. There are also many variations within these basic shapes, and the great variety can only be really appreciated by reference to illustrations.

Although the collector will mostly confine himself to bottle labels, a keen enthusiast will also gather a number of barrel or cask labels. These are mainly circular in shape, of simple design and are usually printed in one colour, the most common being red. With the advent of aluminium casks and kegs, however, there are far fewer interesting cask labels around and small self-adhesive stickers of a bland, tasteless design tend to be used instead, giving little or no scope to the collector.

An impressive array of barrel or cask labels from Wales, England and Ireland. All are over 50 years old and only Macardle, Moore & Company Ltd. of Dundalk still trade.

23

Brewed for the occasion

Everybody likes to drink to celebrate a special occasion. The breweries have not forgotten this, and have issued special brews to commemorate events as divergent as the independence of a new African state, a royal visit, a beer festival, and even the wedding of one of the directors. In particular, the people of Germany drink beer to celebrate most events–from a house-warming party to a major rejoicing. This is reflected in the country's beer labels, which capture the colour and spirit of the various festivals held throughout the land. 'Festbier' labels appear frequently, especially those for the most famous gathering of the year–the Oktoberfest. The traditional drink for this event is 'Märzen', or 'March beer', which is the last of the winter beer which has been brewed a little stronger to make sure that, at the end of the summer, it has been well fermented and is exceptionally strong.

Oktoberfest labels have also been issued outside Germany. Not surprisingly, the South-West Breweries in the former German colony of South-West Africa (now Namibia) introduced a special brew, but less expected was the label issued in 1977 by an English country inn ('The Cross Keys' at Pulloxhill) for a beer produced by the Bedford brewer Charles Wells. Coopers of Adelaide, South Australia is another brewer who has adopted the Oktoberfest habit. Coopers also brew an annual beer for the 'Schützenfest', an event which originates from the time groups of sharpshooters or vigilantes protected towns and villages.

Rejoicings such as carnivals and firework displays have been commemorated on labels. The Carnival Ale brewed by Charles Wells in England to celebrate the Bedford Carnival in 1975 was unique in that the beer was presented to the public in ICI 'Merolite' pouches rather than in bottles or cans. In Britain, major festivals are few and far between: special labels were produced by several British brewers, notably Barclay Perkins, Castletown Brewery and Mann Crossman & Paulin for the Festival of Britain in 1951. Tollemache, brewers of Ipswich, brewed two Festival ales, each bearing identical labels apart from the date when the respective brews were made.

There are also beers suitable for a particular season. Spring is recalled by 'Fruhjährsbock', brewed by the brewery of Fränk Saale at Bad Neustadt, Bavaria, and by 'Spring Ale' from Eldridge Pope of Dorchester, England. Easter is celebrated by a 'Påskebryg' in Scandinavia, and by 'Osterbier' in Germany. 'Summer Pale Ale' from Elgoods of Wisbech, England, with a rather unusual pear-shaped label, represents the second season of the year, and Truswells, another English brewery, now defunct, had an 'October Brew' for Autumn. Winter is illustrated best by the many Christmas beers produced all over the world. In Germany, they are known as 'Weihnachts-bier', while in Scandinavian countries, the 'Julebryg' or 'Jule Øl', with the familiar figure of Santa Claus on the label, is commonplace. All four seasons are remembered by the labels issued by the Bryggeriet Vestfyen in Assens, Denmark, and 'Seasons Brew' by Simonds of Reading, England, conjures up a slightly different aspect of 'season'. This beer, which was abbreviated to 'S.B.', was of a light pale variety, specially brewed to withstand export to warmer countries.

The commemoration of historical events has given rise to many special labels. Many in this category are connected with the development of the brewery itself, such as the company's centenary or bicentenary. Notable examples are the Jubilee labels from the Ceres Brewery, Denmark, the Brauerei Otto Gürth, Weissenfels, Germany and Hall & Woodhouse, Blandford, England. When Guinness of Dublin celebrated their bicentenary in 1959, the special label they issued

Some of the labels released by English brewers in 1951 when they introduced special beers to commemorate the Festival of Britain.

was no different in basic design to their ordinary Extra Stout label but was produced on gold foil rather than the ordinary buff-coloured paper. There was also an additional label on the back, displaying a portrait of Arthur Guinness, the founder, and a gold neck slip. The company went even further in their celebrations. They dropped 150,000 empty, but sealed, bottles into the Atlantic Ocean from 30 different ships over a period of six weeks. Each bottle had embossed upon it 'The World Over 1759–1959. Special Drop Atlantic Ocean to celebrate and commemorate Guinness Bicentenary 1959', and inside was a Foreign Extra Stout label in gold, a story about Guinness,

a message from 'Office of King Neptune' and instructions on how to make a table lamp from the bottle.

The founding fathers and famous brewers of other breweries also have their commemorative labels. Wiibroe's Brewery of Elsinore celebrated its hundred and twenty-fifth anniversary in 1965 when it introduced 'Senior' beer; on the label was a picture of the founder. Carlsberg, on the other hand, celebrated 75 years of the use of pure cultivated yeast in practical brewing by the issue of a label in 1958 depicting the inventor of the method, Emil Christian Hansen. The opening and closure of breweries have also prompted

A time for rejoicing: a selection of labels from breweries in Germany, Scandinavia, England, Australia, Canada, Namibia and the United States which have been designed for brews celebrating festive occasions—especially the Oktoberfest and the Schützenfest.

25

A splendid array of bottle labels issued mainly for the Silver Jubilee of Queen Elizabeth II in 1977. Three 1935 Jubilee labels and one issued for Queen Victoria's Golden Jubilee in 1887 give a historical touch to the display. All 57 label designs used for commercially-produced Silver Jubilee brews are depicted here, although a few minor variations exist.

Right
Brewers have celebrated 30, 50, 70, 100, 125, 150, 200 or 300 year anniversaries of their founding by brewing special beers. Some, like the Faxe Brewery, Courage, Wiibroe's Brewery and Guinness, celebrate their founding fathers, while others issue appropriate brews for the opening or closing of breweries.

Opposite, above
Important events in the development of a nation (especially Independence celebrations), celebrations to mark their anniversaries, and anniversaries of towns, have provided excuses for special beers.

Opposite, below
Victory in war (1945) and in sport (1966) are celebrated by British breweries. Family occasions are remembered too—the marriage of a director of Devenish's Weymouth Brewery in 1973 gave rise to a unique brew, while Greenall Whitley and Randall's Brewery of Jersey have produced special beers for twenty-first birthdays of members of the Greenall family.

special labels: a commemorative label marked the first brew at Whitbread's Luton Brewery, England, in 1969, while eight years before, Tollemache & Cobbold's 'Final Brew' had commemorated a rather disappointing end to the Brook Street Brewery, Ipswich.

Other historical labels celebrate landmarks in the development of a nation. In 1963, Kenya declared independence; a special beer, 'Uhuru' (meaning independence), was brewed by the country's three breweries and 12,500 bottles were given to the Government for presentation at the state and civic balls. Nigerian independence in 1960 led to the issue of not one but three labels

from the small English brewery of Howcrofts. Anniversaries rather than independence were remembered by 'Rhodes Centenary Ale', brewed by Rhodesian Breweries in 1953, and 'Mayflower Ale' produced jointly by Courage and Plymouth Breweries, England, in 1970 to mark the three hundred and fiftieth anniversary of the sailing of the Pilgrim Fathers to America. Other stirring episodes in history are recalled by the 'Celebration Irish Ale', brewed by Beamish & Crawford of Cork in 1966 to celebrate the fiftieth anniversary of the Easter Rising, and the 'St. Edmund Ale' of Greene King of England which, in 1970, commemorated the martyrdom 1,100 years previously of King

Edmund of East Anglia, who was, according to tradition, killed by the Danes because he refused to renounce Christianity.

One or two towns and cities have been honoured by a special beer. Okells and the Castletown Brewery from the Isle of Man combined to produce a brew in 1965 for the centenary of Ramsey, and Carlsberg did likewise two years later, to mark the eight hundredth anniversary of Copenhagen.

Probably the most interesting and colourful special brew labels are those celebrating royal occasions. Coronations and jubilees have provided considerable scope for the beer label designer–and hence for the collector. In the United Kingdom, the labels commemorating the coronations of King George V in 1911, King George VI in 1937 and Queen Elizabeth II in 1953 are definitely some of the most sought after specimens. While the Silver Jubilee of King George V inspired a good number of colourful labels, and that of Queen Elizabeth II in 1977 still more, relatively few examples exist from Queen Victoria's Silver Jubilee in 1887. Brewers have not been slow to commemorate royal weddings. Three Danish brewers introduced special beers for the wedding of Princess Margrette and Prince Henri in 1967, following a similar gesture by English brewers H. & G. Simonds of Reading and Warwicks & Richardson of Newark-on-Trent 20 years earlier for the marriage of Princess Elizabeth to Prince Philip. Wedding anniversaries, investitures and royal visits have inevitably led to the introduction of appropriate brews. The Bass Brewery at Burton-on-Trent, England is particularly proud of the occasions when it has been host to a royal visitor, and all have resulted in famous bottled beers. The first visit, on 22 February 1902, was made by King Edward VII, the second, by Edward, Prince of Wales, came on 23 July 1929, and the unique treble was achieved on 7 June 1978 when Princess Anne honoured the brewery with her presence. Whitbread and Charrington number among other English breweries who can record similar events.

Nowhere in the world is the special event label used more extensively than in New Zealand. The small number of breweries in the country would probably offer little scope for the collector were it not for the wide variety of labels covering every conceivable event. Conferences and conventions, club centenaries and celebrations, early exploration feats, tournaments, band contests, Scottish evenings, jazz festivals, military reunions, sporting competitions, dog trials, old school gatherings, trade fairs–all have fired the imagination of the brewers. But it would be wrong to suggest that New Zealand monopolizes the commemorative label scene in that part of the world. Australian brewers have issued their fair share, especially Coopers of South Australia; one label of particular note appeared in 1974 to mark the re-opening of the Pichi Richi railway in the South Australian Flinders Ranges.

Trade, commerce and tourism also feature on special labels. Beers have been brewed to promote hotels, airlines and shipping lines, and even commercial products. When, in 1954, the Polar

A display fit for a king: coronations, weddings and investitures are among the royal occasions which have prompted brews and labels of a superlative quality.

Labels featuring trade, commerce and tourism from the breweries Faxe and Carlsberg of Denmark, Hook Norton and Bass of England, and Tasmanian Breweries.

route from Copenhagen to Los Angeles was inaugurated by the Scandinavian airline SAS (Scandinavian Airlines System), Carlsberg brewed a 'Polar Beer' for the occasion. And England's Hook Norton Brewery have produced several versions of a special 'Jack Pot Ale' label for a renowned hop insecticide. And the market place too is remembered–when a new shopping centre was opened in Burton-on-Trent, England on 4 July 1965, Bass produced a 'Bargates Ale' for the occasion.

One or two victories are commemorated. The ending of hostilities in 1945 prompted several British breweries to launch a suitable celebration brew. More peaceful triumphs on the sportsfield have been recalled by Watney's 'World Cup Ale' and Higsons' 'World Cup Winners Ale'. Even

A few of the many special event labels which have been issued by brewers in New Zealand, with examples from Australia and Ceylon at the top of the photograph.

family occasions are not overlooked. Greenall Whitley of Warrington have adopted the interesting custom of issuing labels in honour of the twenty-first birthdays of members of the family.

Devenish of Weymouth celebrated the wedding of one of its directors with a special brew: rather amusingly, the label bore a design which anticipated the patter of tiny feet.

Departures from the norm

Unusual things have always had an inbuilt attraction, and beer labels which are a little different from the ordinary are no exception. It has been said that the public are generally more interested in the contents of beer bottles than the packaging, yet some labels are arresting enough to demand a second glance before the contents of the bottle is downed.

Take the beer label which was issued by the Pêcheur Group in France, for example. Instead of the customary wording on the label–the brewer's name, brand of beer and address of the brewery–a completely new style was set when the brewery commissioned artist Jean Cocteau to design a label for its De Luxe Pale Ale '3 Etoiles'. He produced a drawing showing the 'Avois' shooting three stars out of his eyes, adding his signature to complete the label.

Sometimes the unusual extends to a complete set. Childhood memories are evoked by labels issued by the Kongens Bryghus of Copenhagen, which take Hans Christian Andersen's fairy tales as their theme. In a similar vein is the delightful set of diamond-shaped labels issued some 15 years ago by the brewery of Hans Diemer, in Hochstadt, West Germany. Sadly, the brewery is no more.

Occasionally, a label will prompt a smile. Perhaps the most well known American comical examples are the sets issued by the Pittsburgh Brewing Company in the early 1960s for their 'Olde Frothingslosh Beer'. One range comprised 'Teddibly Stout', 'Champain', 'Chiantey', 'Honorable Sockey', 'Hopp Scotch', and 'Schnopps', all of which bore drawings and 'silly' slogans undoubtedly designed to produce a certain response– though it might be argued that here was a rather strange brand of humour. A second more colourful set used photographs featuring a bizarre character in two different guises on each label, and to add to the ridicule, one photograph was printed upside down; the slogans equalled the inspired examples used on the earlier labels. Collectors in New Zealand will recall humorous themes from the 'Provincial Bitter' labels re-

Examples of unusual labels: the Pécheur Brewery's '3 Etoiles', designed by artist Jean Cocteau; the bizarre 'Thirsty Moon' from Germany; Adnam's original Centenary Ale, which was withdrawn after the brewery took a dislike to it; '49 Lager' (the beer brewed on the 49th parallel in Canada); and Marlboro' (one of the beers with the same name as cigarette brands), introduced after the acquisition of the Miller Brewing Company by the tobacco giant Phillip Morris Inc.

leased by the Taranaki Brewery & Cordials Ltd. of New Plymouth, depicting Ferdinand the bull, and christened 'Ferdinand's Ranfurly Brew', and the 'Lulu' labels issued for the French rugby tours, showing a rather festive cow.

Frivolity also features in the 'Merrie Monk' labels of Marstons of Burton-on-Trent, England and the 'Pixie Ale' by the American DuBois Brewing Company. One Danish brewery (Thor of Randers) pictures a comic strip cartoon character familiar to British newspaper readers as Andy Capp, but known to the Danish public as 'Kasket Karl'—the word 'Kasket' meaning a worker's cloth cap, as worn by Andy. Other amusing characters include Ceres Brewery's 'Red Eric', who stares at drinkers of the Danish beer named after him, and the devil himself, colloquially known as 'Old Nick', depicted on the interesting barley wine label by Youngs of Wandsworth, England.

But humour can be presented in a more subtle way, in the form of a pun. John Reid & Company Ltd. of Auckland, New Zealand, had labels which illustrate this very well: they featured two characters called, not surprisingly, 'Tim' and 'Ru' from the town Timaru. This, coupled with the slogan 'Bottled with Loving Care' surely attracted comments from the public. Older examples, from the United Kingdom, are Aitken's 'Nun Nicer Brand' and Crowleys of Hampshire, whose label shows a crow's head. The trade marks of Greene King of Bury St. Edmunds (a

green king) and the Redruth Brewery (with Red Ruth emerging from the cornfield), are more straightforward puns, though the latter was certainly bound to raise a few eyebrows.

From the subtle, we progress to the ridiculous. This is best exemplified by 'Thirsty Moon', a colourful German label from Bremen which pictures an attractive maiden in her night attire offering a drink of beer to the new moon. More

An interesting set of labels from the Kongens Bryghus of Denmark. The drawings depict themes from the fairy tales of Hans Christian Andersen.

Two of the comical sets of labels released in the 1960s by the Pittsburgh Brewing Company in the United States.

Right
The unusual diamond-shaped labels of the brewery of Hans Diemer of Höchstädt, West Germany evoke childhood memories with their fairy-tale themes.

Opposite
Spot the difference: a selection of variations for the collector. The Hansa Brewery labels from Norway highlight extra wording for export purposes; the shield-shaped labels from Pripps Bryggeri, Sweden are different in size; the Georges and Crosswells examples show colour and minor design differences respectively; while one of the labels of the Dyer Meakin Breweries Ltd. in India reveals an overprinting for Defence Services. Bottlers' variations are illustrated by the 1887 labels issued by Samuel Allsopp & Sons of Burton-on-Trent, England; additional wording appears on the top half of one of the labels from the Star Brewery, Eastbourne; and the contents of the bottle has been added to the left-hand example from the Cascade Brewery, Tasmania.

Below
Examples of the 'punning' label: a 'green king'; Red Ruth in the cornfield; Noakes Brown Ale showing the oak tree; the crow's head of Crowleys; Aitken's 'Nun Nicer' brand; and 'Tim and Ru' from Timaru.

down to earth, but still unusual, is the 'Forty Nine Canadian Lager', produced on the forty-ninth parallel at Fort Frances, Ontario. Some North American 'departures from the norm' have arisen as a result of business activity. When the tobacco giant Philip Morris Inc. acquired the Miller Brewing Company of Milwaukee, in 1970, it not only introduced more sophisticated marketing techniques to boost sales but also launched new low calorie brands of beer, some of which were unusual in that they bore the same names as cigarette brands.

If humour attempts to attract the masses, other beers have been reserved for a select few. In this category fall the various experimental brews which may never be promoted on a wide scale, Speight's 'Double Brown' from New Zealand and 'Brad's Special' from Mitchells & Butlers' experimental brewery in Birmingham, England being two that spring to mind. Yet Whitbread's 'Final Selection', originally brewed for the chairman of the company, was eventually appreciated by many others, who were warned to drink the ale with discretion. The labels for these beers are particularly scarce, since the beer has only been around for a short time. Of equal rarity are the temporary or provisional labels which are either issued after a brewery takeover – as in the case of

J. W. Green's 'Anchor Ale' brewed at Grantham and Alford, England – or during a printer's strike, like the McCracken's 'Khaki' Extra Stout label from Carlton & United Breweries, in Melbourne, Australia. Labels in both these categories tend to be pedestrian and unattractive, yet they are nevertheless interesting to the collector.

Some types of labels are of definite interest to others besides the collector. Few men can fail to be impressed by the label featuring a 'pin up'. Unlike beer cans, labels have not tended to verge on the pornographic, although brewers have sometimes been a little cheeky to say the least, and occasionally a scantily-clad young lady will

appear on the bottle. Especially picturesque are the labels of the Brasserie de Tahiti Papeete, showing beautiful South Sea Island 'natives', but other brewers who have featured attractive maidens are the Holsten Brewery, Hamburg, and the Berliner-Weissbier Brauerei. Hackerbräu of Munich preferred a rather generous-looking barmaid. More suggestive was the Smiling Girl on the Dutch label from United Breweries of Amsterdam, and the entertaining lady on the 'Striptis' label from the Czech Pivovarné Laško. But pride of place must go to the devotee of Bacchus, the god of wine: Baccante, with child,

who has adorned the labels of Tollemache's Breweries of Ipswich, England for over 50 years, with only a short break in the early 1970s.

The collector sometimes needs to look carefully at a label to realize that it is indeed unusual. Whether by accident or design, some brewers have issued labels which, from a distance, can be confused with those advertising more famous products. The buff colour used so extensively in the past by Guinness of Dublin has been copied by many brewers all over the world for their Stout labels. A number of firms, in particular the Standard Brewery in New Zealand and the Uruguay Brewery in Montevideo, also included the code figures in the centre of the label which were, up to 1959, so familiar to drinkers of Guinness Extra Stout, and which if reversed revealed the date of bottling. Similar 'protectionist' backgrounds to the one adopted by Bass for its labels to prevent them being copied are also common: the Pale Ale label by the Atlantic Brewery of H. P. Miles & Company in Madeira even used the same colours as the British counterpart. And the similarity between Watney's 'Extra Milk Stout' and the 'Brown Beer' from the Palestine Brewery Ltd. is particularly striking. The 'Double Brown' label from Dominion Breweries Ltd. of Otahuhu,

New Zealand resembles the label from Whitbread of London, the only difference being the colours. And doubtless the enthusiast will find many other examples.

These differences pale into insignificance compared with many variations to the standard design of some labels – variations which include such criteria as size of label, size and style of print, colour, bottlers' names, wording to comply with particular export requirements and bottle contents. These are just some of the differences that add to the fascination of label collecting and to the extensive nature of the hobby.

Above
For a limited period only: labels from three experimental brews.

Opposite, above
Further humorous themes from England, the United States, Holland, Denmark and New Zealand demonstrate that beer drinking has its lighter moments!

Opposite, below
Temporary labels, mainly issued during printers' strikes, while drab in appearance, are among the most difficult labels for the collector to obtain.

Similarities in design can result in some confusion. In this photograph, the serial number and the oval shape characteristic of Guinness, and the protectionist background of Bass, can be seen on labels issued by other companies.

37

The language of labels

Opposite
Labels depicting some of the world's beer styles and types. Berliner Weisse, Bavarian Weizenbier, Düsseldorfer Alt, Kölsch, Bock, Münchener type Dunkel and Märzen all originate from Germany; Spezial-lager comes from Austria; Bitter, Mild, Cooper, Brown Ale, Stingo, Barley Wine, Porter from the British Isles; and Guinness Dublin Stout is in a class of its own. Belgium gives us Scotch, Rodenbach (a red beer), 'Gueuze' and 'Kriek'. Pilsner and Budweiser are famous Czech styles emulated but never equalled elsewhere, while Denmark has Dark and Light White Ale *(Mørkt* and *Lys Hvidtøl)* and Mumme, a roasted malt brew, also popular in Germany. Pale, India Pale (which evolved at Burton-on-Trent) and other weaker variants can be found in most English-speaking countries. Anchor Steam Beer is the only true beer style in the United States.

Below
Some European abbeys still brew beer for sale to the public, and here are some labels issued by the Trappist Monks at Rochefort, southern Belgium.

The saying 'variety is the spice of life' is particularly true of beer. The wide range of different styles and types cannot fail to arouse the interest and stir the imagination of both the beer drinker and labologist. Some beers originate at one brewery and then become household names, such as Pilsener beer from Pilsen, Czechoslovakia; others originate in one particular area or province and then become popular elsewhere, such as the Bock beers first brewed in the Einbeck area of Lower Saxony, Germany, with labels picturing the male goat; yet others are fiercely traditional brews indigenous to various localities or single breweries which can be found nowhere else. Chief amongst the latter are the Belgian specialities like the wild wheat *(lambic)* beers from the Brussels area (sometimes blended to make a fruity beer called 'Gueuze', or a cherry beer called 'Kriek' and the red and white beers found in other parts of Belgium.

Many British styles of beer appear on labels throughout the world. The most popular British style is Bitter Ale, a heavily hopped beer, often called Pale Ale in the United Kingdom today and more of a lager type in Australia. Other Pale, Sparkling or Light Ale labels can be found throughout the English-speaking world. Mild Ale, often advertised on the old barrel labels of draught beer, rarely appears in bottles today. Labels for Stouts, particularly of the Irish variety, are seen in many countries, but those advertising strong ales, barley wines or old ales, are confined to Britain. Porter or 'Entire', which

is said to have originated at the 'Old Blue Last' inn in Curtain Road, Shoreditch, London in the 1700s, provided little scope for the label collector in Britain until 1978, when the Penrhos Court Brewery at Lyonshall, near Kington, Herefordshire reintroduced the brew with an attractive barrel label. In other parts of the world, however, especially in Eastern Europe and North America, Porter continues to be produced on a wider scale and is one of the fine beers of the Anchor Steam Brewing Company in San Francisco, whose labels are particularly sought after by collectors. The only indigenous beer style in the United States is its most celebrated brew: Steam Beer. Germany on the other hand, has many styles: apart from Bock and Doppelbock, there are dark and light Munich beers *(dunkel* and *hell)*, Weizenbier from Bavaria and Berliner Weisse, Dortmunder-type beers, Kölsch from Cologne and Düsseldorfer Alt. All have given rise to many varied and colourful labels.

Beer styles are only one of many themes for the beer label collector to pursue. The discerning enthusiast will perceive that many brewers are anxious to include old brewing traditions. And the history of brewing in countless towns and cities is closely linked with their abbeys and monasteries. In Burton-on-Trent, the English town which has no equal for beer, the abbots of Burton were brewing in 1295, long before the coming of the commercial brewers who were to make the town famous. Some abbeys still perpetuate these links: about twelve abbeys in Germany, five in Belgium and one in Holland brew beer on the premises today. The beer labels issued by the Trappist abbey at Rochefort, Belgium may not be spectacular in their design or use of colour, but the labologist will be fascinated by them. A few other Belgian abbeys have ceased to brew themselves but have kept up the tradition by coming to an arrangement with commercial brewers for the production of a special ecclesiastical brew. All these brews will naturally have labels featuring monks, abbeys and churches, which are a popular motif for other beers.

A most attractive set of labels depicting Ely Cathedral was issued by the Forehill Brewery, Ely, England, in the 1950s. In 1968, the same brewery recalled links with the church when it produced 'Bona Cervisia', a revival of the monastic brew made 600 years previously, to celebrate the feast of St. Etheldreda, patron Saint of Ely

Labels from breweries with long histories. The Bayerische Staatsbrauerei at Weihenstephan, Bavaria, was founded in 1040; the breweries at Třeboň and Podkováň in Czechoslovakia in 1379 and 1434 respectively; and America's oldest concern, D.G. Yuengling at Pottsville, much later in 1829. Tomson & Wotton of Ramsgate was once Britain's oldest brewery, having been founded in 1634, but that distinction now goes to Morland of Abingdon, established in 1711, as Tomson & Wotton has now been taken over.

Cathedral. Beer was in fact brewed in the cathedral precincts by the verger until well into the nineteenth century, when Bishop Harvey Goodwin terminated the practice.

History provides a common theme for labels. In a previous chapter the commemoration of historical events was mentioned; specific periods in a nation's past are also recalled. The Cerveceria Cuauhtemoc S.A. in Mexico, for example, depicts a notable Aztec warrior who was murdered during the destruction of the Indian civilization by the Spanish under the conqueror Hernan Cortés in the sixteenth century. A Cuban brewery, Compania Ron Bacardi, S.A., portrays another 'native' on its 'Cerveza Hatuey' label. The American Indian appears on the labels of several American breweries, as well as on some French and English examples. Soldiers have also provided inspiration, and examples range from the musketeer from Harboe, the Danish brewery, to the more aggressive warlord on the attractive label from the German Brauhaus Garmisch.

Labels from very old breweries have a considerable fascination. The world's oldest is believed to be the Bayerische Staatsbrauerei in Weihenstephan, Bavaria, which was founded way back in 1040. The oldest brewery in the United States, D. G. Yuengling & Son Inc. of Pottsville, Philadelphia, established in 1829, seems a newcomer by comparison. Britain can boast at least a century's headway: Morland of Abingdon, founded in 1711, is the oldest independent brewery and still trades under its original name. Yet Czechoslovakia, with its marvellous brewing tradition, can reach even further back: the brewery at Třeboň, near the Austrian border, dates from 1379, the one at Podkováň from 1434, and another at Rakovnik from 1454.

One permutation on the history theme are the traces of mythology and folklore that are invariably interwoven with the history of a nation. One mythological animal that makes an interesting subject is the dragon, a fine example being the ceremonial beast on the beautifully-balanced Singha Lager Beer label from the Boon Rawd Brewery Company Ltd. in Bangkok. The spirit of the Far East is also captured on the superb labels of the Kirin Brewery of Japan, which show the

Coats of arms introduce superb use of colour and intricate detail into these beer labels from Belgium, England, Norway, Holland, Luxembourg, West Germany, Austria, Scotland, Mexico, and the Congo.

mythical creature which is half horse, half dragon. On the other side of the world, the legend of St. George and the dragon has inspired the design of several labels, and even the name 'Drachenblut' (Dragon's Blood) on one West German label (although this name is by no means unique, having been used by J. W. Green of Luton,

England). Another strange dragon-like creature appears on the labels of the Union Brewery of Yugoslavia. Several griffins have also been noticed, especially on the labels of two famous London breweries: Fuller Smith & Turner and Reids Brewery Company. The phoenix – the mythical bird which rises from the ashes and which

symbolizes eternal life – is popular with breweries the world over, from Ireland to Australia, from Holland to Mauritius.

Other mythical animals, such as unicorns, often appear in the form of heraldic devices on labels, and some truly magnificent examples of these have been released by brewers. It seems a pity that such colourful works of art are only for the beer bottle! Several brewery companies with the name of a city or town use that town's coat of arms on their labels, whilst other brewers have honoured their town by an occasional brew bearing a similar label.

What other motifs have been used by the beer

Birds from all over the world: cockerels, swans, parrots, eagles, a condor, an emu, a bantam, a tui, a capercaillie, a kingfisher, a raven, a falcon, an Aylesbury duck, a goldcrest and a swallow.

The influence of mythology on beer labels around the world. The griffin (or gryphon), phoenix, kirin and dragon (both two- and four-legged varieties) have all provided inspiration for the beer label designer.

Holland. Neither is man's best friend forgotten: the Perth Brewery in Canada and Bernards Brewery in Edinburgh, Scotland have paid tribute to the loyalty of the dog. A few pigs and cows (the latter on Milk Stout labels), a badger, a fox, lambs and rams, bears, spiders, bees and beetles, all contribute to this vast menagerie.

Birds are almost as numerous, and include peacocks, swans, ducks, cockerels, parrots, several eagles, a condor, falcons, an emu and a goldcrest. Trees and flowers are occasionally seen, but brewers generally prefer to illustrate the basic ingredients of beer – hops and barley. Geographical features such as waterfalls, mountains or glaciers, have also inspired the beer label designer. The waterfall is especially popular: Adolph Coors Company of Golden, Colorado accompanies a picture of one with the slogan 'brewed with pure rocky mountain spring water', while the 'Rainbow' label from Kootenay Breweries in British Columbia features a Canadian waterfall in a pine forest, complete with salmon leaping high out of the water. The labels of the Cascade Brewery of Tasmania are aptly illustrated with another wonder of nature. Probably the most picturesque of recent labels showing scenic views is the set with full colour photographs produced by the Leopard Brewery of Hastings, New Zealand in 1977, primarily for Vacation Hotels Ltd.

Man-made landmarks, such as buildings, bridges and statues, have also been illustrated on the beer label. Public buildings are very popular, particularly with Russian brewers; other countries, such as Czechoslovakia and Austria, prefer to portray a cluster of buildings. Castles are a firm favourite too. Tooths of Sydney have featured the Harbour Bridge which has made the city famous, and the South Holland Brewery has showed the Peace Palace at The Hague built after the 1907 Peace Conference from funds largely contributed by Andrew Carnegie, the American millionaire. An interesting issue from the Danish brewers Carlsberg in 1963 celebrated the fiftieth anniversary of Copenhagen's most famous landmark 'Den Lille Havfrue' ('The Little Mermaid'), which was presented to the city by the brewer Carl Jacobsen, the founder of the New Carlsberg Brewery. Also from Denmark is the colourful range of labels from the Odin Brewery at Viborg, in Northern Jutland, and a similar but smaller series from the Lolland Falsters Brewery in Nykøbing, both showing landscape scenes. Incidentally, this Danish brewery has probably originated more themes on beer labels than any other company.

Patriotism and national sentiment are a rich source of themes. The Lolland Falsters Brewery, several Polish brewers and the Cerveceria Nacional in Quezaltenango, Guatemala have all depicted national costumes. Flags have been shown; there are examples from South America and Belgium, while British loyalty is reflected in the label issued by Brakspears of Henley-on-Thames for their 'All British Beer'.

Perhaps even more noticeable than national pride is chauvinism on the part of the brewery business. Countless brewers have adopted the

label designer? Nature provides part of the answer, and all creatures great and small from the five continents have added interest and colour to the products of the breweries. The wildlife of Africa has probably inspired the most labels in this category – lions, elephants, camels, giraffes, antelopes and buffaloes add up to a veritable Noah's ark. As would be expected goats are commonplace on German, Austrian and North American beer labels, and Löwenbräu of Munich have combined goat and lion on a jovial-looking Heller Bock label. Tigers appear on labels by Malayan Breweries in the Far East and by the Richmond N. S. Brewing Company, Australia, and the leopard has been used in New Zealand. Their less fierce relative, the cat, has also featured, the best example being the well designed 'Old Tom' label by Robinsons of Stockport, England. Horses of many breeds appear, from the majestic Suffolk punches on the fine labels of Adnams of Southwold, on England's east coast, to the three grey beasts shown on the Pilsner Beer label from the Cambrinus Brewery of

Labels that bear witness to the fascination of the 'home-brewed' houses in Germany and England. Many establishments in England have ceased to brew although the inn remains, but 'The Three Tuns' at Bishop's Castle still thrives, and occasionally produces a bottled brew. Germany's most renowned 'home-brewed' house (Pinkus Müller's in Münster) is represented by two main and one auxiliary label, with two from Ferdinand Schumacher's 'Golden Kettle' in Düsseldorf, and one (the only kind issued) from 'Im Füchschen' in the same city. Home bottlers in Australia and New Zealand are represented by two hotels with their own special label.

practice of illustrating their premises on labels and some are most impressive. The older labels may exaggerate the size of the undertaking, but the detail can be superb, especially on the early British labels issued by Fordhams of Ashwell and Walter Morgan of Wrotham, both of which even include the horse-drawn brewery waggons in the foreground. But pride does not end there: once a prize is won for a brewery's products, especially at a famous world exhibition, the beer drinker must be told. And what better way to depict the winning cup or gold medal than on the label?

Some brewers never seek to win prizes, but their products are still worthy of renown. Few concerns can better capture the imagination of the beer connoisseur and labologist alike than the 'home-brewed' inns of England, Germany and Czechoslovakia. Up to the fifteenth century, in England at least, all beer sold to the public was brewed by the ale-house keeper on his premises or in a small brewhouse adjoining. This tradition is still maintained by a few houses. In the green, undulating countryside near the Welsh border lies the sleepy Shropshire town of Bishop's Castle, which contains probably the most famous 'home-brewed' house in the land – 'The Three Tuns'. The inn, established before 1642, was owned by the Roberts family until 1976, when it was sold to Mr Peter Milner, who continues the tradition. As in most 'home-brewed' houses, the beer is on draught; nevertheless 'The Three Tuns' has issued some interesting bottle and barrel labels, the former portraying the brewhouse in the yard. Of the other eight (three original and five new) 'home-brewed' houses in existence in England today, only one, 'The Masons Arms' at Southleigh, near Witney, has bottled its beers. Yet in the past this was the practice for many inns – at Shaftesbury, Stafford, Leeds, Hockley Heath, Wolverhampton, Southwick and Nottingham. The 'home-brewed' house at Nottingham, 'Ye Olde Trip to Jerusalem', was, until it ceased brewing about 1939, the oldest of its kind, having been established below the castle walls in 1189.

Germany, too, has a tradition of home brewing. The most celebrated example is Pinkus Müller's

Scenic views on labels from the Leopard Brewery of Hastings, New Zealand, released in 1977.

Brewers are not slow to exploit the awards they have won at exhibitions for the purposes of labology, and have designed some fine labels as a consequence.

establishment in Münster, which was founded in 1816. The beers have proved competitive with those of larger brewers and have won prizes. Düsseldorf is unique in having three 'home-brewed' houses: Zum Üerige, Im Füchschen, and Ferdinand Schumacher. But even these cannot compare with Prague's only remaining home brewery – U Fleků, which is also a famous beer cellar where many gather to drink the famous brews produced on the premises. Not in the same category, for they are home-bottlers rather than home-brewers, are the hotels that bottle beer produced by the large breweries in Australia and New Zealand, but they are worth mentioning as they have produced some interesting labels.

Like stamps, beer labels depict an infinite number of themes. One brewery (Gränges Bryggarn of Grängesberg, Sweden) introduced a set of labels in 1974 illustrating different trades; another, Karlsberg Brauerei K. G. Weber of Homburg Saar, West Germany, turned to transport when it portrayed a range of old vehicles in 1965. This theme was resurrected by Harboes Bryggeri in Denmark ten years later, and the range of old vehicles was extended. Ships and the sea, and nautical devices generally, have been much more popular, probably because the ship has always been essential for export. The Danish 'Ship's Ale' (Skibsøl) was originally a strong, well hopped beer specially brewed to withstand long journeys, but today it is a very different concoction, dark and with little alcohol.

Low alcohol or 'near beers' have been produced in many countries, particularly during Prohibition in the United States. But other nations have also experienced temperance periods, especially Britain, where, during the First World War, many breweries and mineral water manufacturers produced a range of non-intoxicating beers under the various names 'Hop Ale', 'Hop Bitters', 'Dinner

A selection of labels promoting sport and other pastimes. Included here are two which recall the Olympic Games, and a set by the Dortmund Actien Brauerei of West Germany which cover a whole range of recreational pursuits.

Non-alcoholic or near-beers are favoured in some countries, while in others, there have been temperance periods when such beers were promoted.

Ale', 'Kops Ale', 'Oatmeal Stout', and 'Victoria Ale', the latter from Fremlins of Maidstone. More recent examples include Tuborg's 'Bov Brew', Pabst 'Tonic' from the United States, 'Central Malt Beer' from the United Breweries of Copenhagen, and the occasional examples produced for Saudi Arabia where alcohol is banned. Iceland produces little else apart from 'near beers' or malt extract.

Many malt beers of low alcoholic content extol the virtues of a healthy existence. For example, 'Kraftperle' Maltzbier produced by the Dortmunder-Actien-Brauerei in West Germany has a set of labels featuring different sports. Sport is also the theme of the label issued as part of another set by the Consorcio de Cervecerias Bavaria of Columbia to mark that country's participation in the World Cup in 1962. Boxing is also covered: 'Birra Moretti' from Italy and 'For Top' from the Solibra Brasserie in Abidjan in the Ivory Coast are interesting examples. And the Olympic Games are represented by the Vorterøl label from Frydenlund of Oslo and the Olympic Lager issued by Allsopps (East Africa). A more intellectual pastime is promoted by the Swedish Malmö Förenade Bryggerier with its 'Chess' label, and in England, the checkerboard is still the trade mark of Wilsons Brewery of Manchester.

Practical collecting

As a schoolboy nearly fifteen years ago, I decided to go on a bicycle trip through the Cotswolds – one of the most picturesque areas in England. At that time, my fascination with label collecting was just beginning. It had grown through an interest in my home town of Maidstone in the hop county of Kent, in its industry, and in particular, its breweries. I gathered the labels from these local firms as mementoes, and soon became curious about breweries in other towns and villages and wanted to collect their labels too. And so, having mapped out a route which took in a good few country breweries, I embarked on an adventure and, despite the vagaries of the English weather, gained a fascinating insight into the operation of a traditional industry. I visited breweries in Oxford, Witney, Burford, Stow-on-the-Wold, Hook Norton and Banbury, and returned via other establishments in Northampton and Bedford. The first glimpse of the grey-stone buildings of the Donnington Brewery, complete with water wheel and fine pond with exquisite water fowl, nestling in a Cotswold valley, near Stow-on-the-Wold, is something I shall never forget. The quaintness of this tiny brewery, which supplies only 17 public houses, did much to spur my interest in my new hobby. And my fascination grew as I obtained labels of a different design to add to the nucleus of my collection.

This anecdote is to show that a label collector who visits a brewery in search of labels will, if he shows a keen interest, be rewarded. There may be a few concerns unlikely to issue labels, but generally speaking, brewers are most helpful. Yet it should be emphasized that they are under no obligation to comply with collectors' requests, for running a business is demanding. At some larger firms it may be difficult to get through the main gate, especially with the growing accent on security, but usually a call at the office results in some degree of success. Ideally, a chat with the Bottling Manager or a member of his staff is a good way of getting hold of not only current labels but also some obsolete ones too. Unfortunately, many brewers tend to destroy out-of-date labels to avoid confusion with more modern examples which are required to comply with various regulations governing contents and country of origin. If you can manage to get hold of a member of staff who has the time to spare, he may be able to direct you to an attic or an old store where old, discarded samples can be found. Above all, always be polite and remember that brewery staff are more than likely to be very busy people.

Politeness is also the key to contact by correspondence. Most breweries will reply to a request for labels if a stamped, addressed envelope or International Reply Coupon is enclosed, but one or two have found that dealing with requests has resulted in too much work and have stopped supplying their advertising material by post. The addresses of breweries are fairly easy to find: usually, the labologist societies will help, and information can be gleaned from the appropriate trade directories. Arrangements with label collecting organizations to distribute labels to members have sometimes been made by brewers, especially by those reluctant to reply to written requests.

While most labels can be obtained direct from the breweries in mint condition, some collectors still prefer to buy a bottle of beer, drink the contents and soak the label from the bottle. But this method has drawbacks: it is expensive and is usually impracticable unless the collector is a keen traveller or specializes in a small range. Moreover, some breweries use such strong glues

Labels depicting botanical themes. Although trees and flowers are used by some brewers, particularly as trade marks, more often it is the basic ingredients of beer that are illustrated.

these days that it can be a considerable task for even the most dedicated enthusiast to remove the label, which can be badly damaged in the process.

Occasionally, a collection of labels, or individual samples, are offered for sale. Those collectors who are members of a labologists' organization are most likely to benefit here, as such sales are mainly advertised in the societies' publications, although the weekly advertisers, such as the British 'Exchange & Mart', have labels for sale from time to time. Old collections are few and far between, however. The beer label, unlike the postage stamp, is unfortunately more likely to be destroyed because people are unaware of its worth. Yet although beer labels will never assume the enormous value that rare stamps do, the label collector will not obtain additions to his collection without some cost, for it has been realized that there must be some kind of mechan-

ism to distinguish the rare examples from the more common ones. Auctions, which are held occasionally, especially in England, are not always advisable as label prices tend to be inflated and some collectors find that certain labels are out of their reach.

Probably the most common way of building a collection, apart from visiting or writing to breweries, is by exchanging duplicate labels with fellow collectors. The various labologist societies throughout the world all further this method by holding meetings or by encouraging members to correspond. Meetings, which can be conducted on an area or on an international basis, provide a useful opportunity for bartering. Most exchanging, however, is done by post, and the majority of the newsletters or publications issued by the beer label collecting organisations have space for members to advertise their require-

Two sets of labels from Danish brewers, one from the Odin Brewery at Viborg, and the other from the Lolland Falsters Brewery, Nykøbing.

Grängesbryggarn of Sweden feature traditional occupations on this set of labels issued in 1974.

All creatures great and small: a fine international selection of labels featuring animals as divergent as the bee, the squirrel, the lion and the crocodile.

Landscape scenes, especially mountains, waterfalls and glaciers, are popular with brewers and make an attractive label.

From horse drawn to motorized transport: three breweries, two in Germany, one in Denmark, with different styles but a common theme. The Danish labels are part of a larger set produced for the Irma supermarket chain.

ments and their offers. Generally, exchanging is conducted on a one-to-one basis, on the assumption that the labels are of the same vintage, but the newly-established collector may find himself at a disadvantage if a fellow enthusiast has a considerably larger collection of duplicates. There must obviously be an element of 'fair trading' in exchanges, which also depend on the generosity of the individual collector.

These, then, are the established avenues for the collector to pursue. Yet a collection may never be enhanced unless the enthusiast is prepared to research his subject well, and to apply dedication to his search for labels, leaving no stone unturned. Old buildings which have remained empty and sometimes derelict since brewing ceased there are the most likely source of old labels, providing there is no difficulty in entry and that the necessary consent has been obtained. Labels have in the past been discovered in the most out-of-the-way places. A few have come to light in cellars of inns, or during demolition of breweries or bottling stores. Printers' guard books have sometimes proved an interesting source of obsolete labels but it is one which, with the growing popularity of the hobby, may possibly have been exhausted. Contact with ex-directors of brewery companies, and former employees, has also brought its rewards. Letters to newspapers and the occasional feature on the hobby in a periodical with a fairly large circulation have also been beneficial. In short, every conceivable angle is worth exploring.

A few of the many labels depicting man-made landmarks. Some, like Windsor Castle, Copenhagen's 'Little Mermaid', Sydney Harbour Bridge, the Peace Palace in The Hague, and the twin towers of the 15th-century Gothic Frauenkirke, Munich, are especially famous.

Patriotic beer labels from Great Britain, Belgium, Honduras, Guatemala, Peru and Ecuador.

Once the enthusiast has collected a number of labels he will need to consider how to store them. Some collectors affix the labels to large sheets, exhibition boards or thin card, and others merely keep fairly haphazard scrapbooks, but a more systematic way of collecting is to mount the labels in loose-leaf albums, where pages can be added to allow for expansion of a collection. There are various types of albums: ring binders are quite popular but one disadvantage is the need for the paper inserts to be punched; lever-arch files operate on the same principle but are considered by many to be too bulky. Photograph albums are used by some collectors but the number of pages is usually restricted and they tend to be expensive. Probably the best album is a spring-back binder containing a flexible or elastic spine to allow easy release of the loose-leaf sheets. The size of binder is a matter of individual preference and will probably depend on the size of the bookshelf where the albums are to be stored. Paper inserts of any colour can be used, although most collec-

National costumes make an interesting theme. The top five labels are from Polish breweries; the centre label is a superb example from Guatemala, while the label from Noakes of London (which ceased trading in 1930) depicts Scottish costumes. The remaining labels, issued by the Lolland Falsters Brewery, Denmark, are part of a larger set featuring regional costumes.

tors prefer white bond paper. Labels can then be mounted with good quality stamp hinges. The use of glue or adhesive tape is not recommended; it makes rearrangement of pages to accommodate additional labels difficult, and can result in a damaged label, which not only devalues the collection but reduces its exchange value in the event of a better example being found.

There are different ways of arranging labels in your collection. They can be placed in alpha-

betical order of breweries under each country, county or region. Some collectors, however, prefer to file in brewery group order, reflecting the development, in terms of mergers and acquisitions, of a major company. Ideally, labels should be arranged in chronological order, or if the collector's knowledge in this sphere is limited, in set sequence.

It was once common practice for collectors to advertise by putting their name and address on

54

the reverse of duplicate labels by means of a rubber stamp. Too often, however, this led to the defacement of a label, especially when too much ink was applied to the rubber stamp. Most societies advise against this method of advertising.

The hints given above are all fundamental to the new collector. Further detailed guidance is readily available from any labologist society. Some have made a start on cataloguing all known beer labels, but to do this for all the labels in the world would be a massive task.

Beer label collecting is not undertaken for commercial reasons and is by and large purely a spare-time occupation, and so the collector's knowledge of the range and number of labels which have been issued is somewhat limited. But then discovering hitherto unknown labels is part of the fascination of this interesting and absorbing hobby which commends itself to young and old alike in all parts of the world.

A superb selection of Guinness labels issued around 1900 for export to various parts of the world, and very different from the firm's later labels, on which the standard colours of buff and black are used.

BEER MATS & COASTERS
The collecting craze

Are you a tegestologist? And before you think it's a perverse activity let me assure you that it is the name formally given to collectors of beer mats or coasters. The name is derived from the Latin 'teges', which literally means a covering or mat. Collectors are sometimes affectionately called dripsomaniacs for obvious reasons.

What tempts people to start collecting is difficult to establish, but I have always maintained that whatever your normal interests, someone, somewhere, sometime has issued a mat or mats which you would find interesting and might wish to keep. When you consider that mats have been issued by all manner of firms advertising every imaginable beer and alcoholic drink, non-alcoholic drink, all sorts of transport companies, the Royal Society for the Prevention of Accidents (ROSPA), the National Coal Board (NCB), TV dealers, greyhound tracks, circuses, publishers, restaurants, seaside resorts, golf clubs, banks, estate agents etc., you get the picture.

Many series of mats have been issued over the years featuring sailing ships, hot air balloons, tips on skiing, olympic sports, old drinking vessels, flowers, gardening hints, wild life, sporting records, beauty spots, historical events, counties, countries, recipes, cocktails, modes of transport, fashions, greyhounds, horses, inn signs, wild animals, golfing stars, crosswords, pin-up girls, deep sea fishing boats, riddles, pub games, country crafts, unusual pastimes, royal naval vessels, towns, Royal Air Force insignia, fairy stories, cheeses, puzzles, football teams, famous paintings, Scottish clan tartans, astronauts, TV characters, history of beer, brewing, chocolate, breweries, landmarks etc., etc., and an inexhaustible range of comic characters, cartoons and jokes and it seems probable that out of all these, something should interest you.

Since they can be acquired freely, a number of people maintain that beer mats have no value. Since the mats are designed to be disposable, they are very often thrown away before the collector has a chance to obtain any, and this creates a demand. Wherever there is a demand for an item in short supply a value will be established by normal market conditions.

I have often been told that my mats are worthless compared, for example, with stamps; but I maintain that whereas any stamp can be obtained if you can pay the price, a number of the older beer mats are still probably unknown to the collecting fraternity. Owning a very rare beer mat gives a special kind of satisfaction, since the chances of other collectors obtaining a copy is extremely remote.

Values of mats depend on rarity and hence one has to beware of fakes. Unfortunately several years ago a printer on the continent reprinted old mats specifically to sell to collectors, and if the

56

original plates are used and the material looks right, these fakes are difficult to detect. Luckily there are chemical methods available for assessing the age of a mat, so deliberate fraud can be detected. All collectors should be very wary of any large batches of very old mats which suddenly come to light. A mat may appear which is a variation of the design of an existing mat – for example, a colour may be changed, or a double-sided version of a single-sided mat may be issued. Often attempts have been made to fake variation mats by the use of a felt-tip pen to change a colour, or by splitting a mat in two with a razor blade.

It is a pity that some collectors seem to encourage this kind of activity by trying to claim that minor differences in fact make different mats. These small difference freaks, as they are called, do not appreciate the practicalities of present day mat printing, where variations on the size of mat frequently occur due to one cutter being slightly different from the rest. Colour shades also vary, depending on whether the ink has just been made or is a day old and running thin, and also whether the board is bone dry or slightly moist. Since even opening the door to the printing shop can affect things, it seems a bit extreme to expect every mat in, say, a seven- or ten-day run to be absolutely identical.

While there are now a number of societies around the world catering for the mat collector and breweriana enthusiast, the oldest English-speaking society and the largest is the British Beermat Collectors Society, abbreviated to BBCS. The BBCS was founded in 1960 by Chris Walsh, who placed an advertisement in the 'Exchange & Mart' magazine asking other collectors to contact him. An enthusiastic response gave birth to the

From top to bottom: the three Whiteweys nursery rhyme mats, three of the club puzzles; and the series of six Squires gin mats depicting the squire of Osbaldeston.

Part of the attractive Van Der Stock Brewery series from Brussels showing early sailing vessels.

The Merchtem Brouwerij Ginder Ale puzzles and a few of the attractive Falkenbier mats.

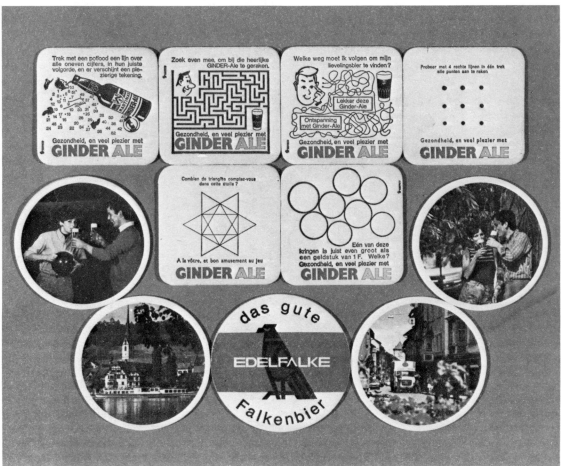

BBCS. The initial 20 members have grown to over 1,200 all over the world. For the first 13 years of its existence the society had as its joint presidents the British comedians Eric Morecambe and Ernie Wise, which no doubt helped it to establish itself. The aim of the BBCS is to further and encourage the interest, knowledge and activities of amateur mat collectors in Britain and throughout the world.

The BBCS issues a monthly beer mat magazine and organizes local meetings all over the United Kingdom each month and a national meeting which is held annually. Each year it supports a charity and in 1978 donated £1,400 to the 1978 Lords Taverners Appeal for youth. Since the Lords Taverners president was Eric Morecambe, it was only natural that he should be presented with the cheque in the form of a giant beer mat measuring 852 mm by 426 mm (33.5 in by 16.7 in). This brought its charitable donations up to £5,000, a truly remarkable achievement. This figure was raised by the generosity of the brewers, other commercial companies and the individual collectors who also donated material and, equally if not more important, their time.

The BBCS issues an individual membership mat for each year, as well as congratulations mats to members whose collections have reached 500, 1,000, 2,000, 3,000 and so on. The largest British collection belongs to Solly Teff who has in the region of over 38,000 but an Austrian collector, Leo Pisker, has the world record of approximately 70,000, that is, over four miles of beer mats (if they are placed in a line end to end).

If you hear cries of 'mats down' in a pub, it's not an orgy, it's simply a group of BBCS members challenging each other to prove their identity. This is simply done by showing your membership mat. For those unable to comply, a donation to society funds is expected.

Each year the BBCS holds a competition amongst breweries to find the BBCS mat of the year, and gives a 'brain of beer mats' award. It also gives a collector of the year award, a gold-plated beer mat which is a unique and highly cherished trophy. And have you ever heard of a mat sandwich? No, well you are forgiven. It is the name given to a competition held at BBCS meetings where a number of mats are sandwiched into a parcel and wrapped in brown paper. The person who guesses the correct number of mats in the parcel, or who gets the closest, wins the mats. This is not always that easy since clever organizers have resorted to including things like house bricks to make it slightly more difficult.

The BBCS has produced catalogues to list all recorded British mats, and also has its own museums. It is currently working on a fully illustrated catalogue of all British brewery mats issued to date. It is largely due to the assistance of the breweries and printers and to the hard work of its members that such a considerable amount of information is available about British mats. Unfortunately, it is only the German societies that have also undertaken such an enormous task to date.

A selection of scenes from all over the world from Becks. This series has been re-issued over the years with a slightly changing common reverse.

History of the beer mat

Opposite, above
Examples of the effectiveness of mats as advertising material: a display of mats advertising not only drinks, but also other concerns, from snuff to safety campaigns (not to mention the British GPO's famous Buzby). Also shown are mats issued by drip mat printers.

Opposite, below
This group includes two 'firsts': E. Lacon & Company's from 1959 and Higsons from 1953. The other mats include a Tennents mat (cut in such a way that it can be used as a winding spool), the standard and mini versions of the Whiteways mat, as well as the Trumans coronation mat (1953).

Beer mats or coasters are perhaps more accurately described as drip mats because all sorts of firms, and not just breweries, use them to promote their products. They are an extremely cost effective method of advertising as they stay a long time in one place where they can be seen – in the home, office, workshop or pub – and yet they are relatively cheap to produce.

The forerunner of the drip mat was the porcelain or pottery tankard stand mainly used to prevent heated tankards of mulled ale from scorching the ale house table tops. These pot stands, or bottle coasters as they were also called, are believed to have given the name 'coaster' to the drip mats in use today, particularly in Australia, New Zealand and also in North America. (Drip mats are 'Sous-bocks' to our French counterparts, and 'Bierdeckel' to our German ones.)

The first wood pulp drip mat was patented in 1892 by Robert Sputh in Dresden, Germany, and mats have been issued in Europe ever since. It is not known exactly when mats first appeared in the United Kingdom, North America and Australasia, but it seems fairly certain that around 1900 would be correct for America and 1920 for the United Kingdom. The first mats believed to be

issued in England were by Watney, Combe, Reid and Company Ltd., advertising Watney's Pale Ale and Reids Stout. These early mats tended to be made of thick embossed board (approximately 3 mm to 4 mm, 0.1 in to 0.15 in) and with small regularly spaced pits or indentations all over its surface. When the edge is examined it is usual to find small slit-like splits where the mat has not been completely compressed. Quite often the printer's name, for example Abbott Brown, Hancor or Regicor (Reginald Corfield), can be found on mats up to the late 1940s. Mats of this period up to 5 mm (0.2 in) thick can be found but usually with the name of the printer just as 'foreign'. Mats 2 mm to 3 mm (0.07 in to 0.1 in) thick and on heavily embossed board but without a printer's name were also issued during this early period. This type of board continued in use until the early 1960s, although the trend was for thinner and smoother mats all the time.

One set of mats issued by Worthington and Company Ltd. in 1961 and depicting six different great men can be found in both embossed board and smooth board varieties. Perhaps the most famous of the British pre-war mats are the single-coloured line drawings of pubs issued by both Bass, Ratcliffe & Gretton Ltd. and Worthington

Some pre-war British brewery mats including Southam's first mat from 1935 and six of the line drawings of pubs issued by Bass and Worthington.

and Company Ltd. in the years 1936 to 1938.

The printer's name can be a valuable aid to giving a mat an approximate date. For example since Abbott Brown ceased production in about 1936 and Charles Tresises in about 1956, mats carrying their name must have been issued before these years. Other printers whose names can be found are Salesprint and Quarmby; both of these are still in business as are Regal Mats, Absorbent Drip Mats, Print and Paper, Ad Mats and a number of smaller printers.

Unfortunately most brewers and mat producing companies do not keep a comprehensive record of the mats they have issued and this means that accurate dating of early mats is not possible. Intelligent guesswork has therefore to be used and by looking at the style of advertising or the trade mark or company name an approximate date can be established. One company which has kept formal records is the Imperial Tobacco Group who have been allocating specific numbers to all their advertising materials since 1905. The Imperial mats which advertise cigarettes, tobaccos and a number of tandems all carry a small code number, such as I.T.C. 8769 or 22211 and can therefore be accurately dated from the following table.

Year	I.T.C. Number	*Any out-of-sequence numbers used in that year*
1930	6708–7185	5131, 5505, 6700
1931	7188–7711	
1932	7720–8367	
1933	8387–8915	
1934	8925–9522	8902
1935	9545–10099	
1936	10136–10724	10749
1937	10732–11330	
1938	11332–11920	11316, 11317, 11318, 11324
1939	11926–12421	
1940	12422–12487	
1946*	12609–12992	
1947	13030–13494	12641
1948	13499–13852	12644
1949	13856–14130	
1950	14150–14503	
1951	14535–14857	
1952	14859–15223	
1953	15234–15598	
1954	15612–16136	
1955	16138–16636	
1956	16657–17122	
1957	17136–17616	
1958	17622–18222	
1959	18236–18802	
1960	18816–19489	
1961	19501–20095	
1962	20101–20633	
1963	20637–21132	
1964	21143–21581	
1965	21589–22322	
1966	22324–22690	
1967	22691–23164	
1968	23165–23454	
1969	23455–23888	
1970	23889–24194	
1971	24195–24652	
1972	24657–25050	
1973	25051–25359	

*N.B. No mats were issued during the Second World War.

(Tandem is the name given to mats which advertise two products, for example Van Dyck cigars and Tuckers ales.)

As boards have become smoother and thinner, they have also become brighter and whiter, and this in turn has meant that a whole new technology in printing methods has evolved. Whereas older mats were printed one mat one colour, one side at a time, modern mats are generally produced one different colour each side 72 at a time. This improved technology has resulted in the very attractive, highly colourful mats of the present day.

Mats tend to reflect the mood of the day and in their own unique way record history. Historical events are recorded on mats, and by looking at the mats of a decade or so ago the different styles in fashion can be seen. Brewery history especially is reflected. For example, when Courage & Company Ltd. merged with Barclay, Perkins & Company Ltd. in 1955, mats which had previously had only the trade mark of a cockerel or Dr Johnson respectively now carried both, since the trading style had become Courage & Barclay Ltd. When this company in turn merged in 1960 with H. & G. Simonds Ltd., the mats then bore the name Courage, Barclay & Simonds Ltd. After a few years the 'Barclay & Simonds Ltd.' was

Left
Foam, felt and wood pulp giant mats, including the Threllfalls jigsaw mats.

Opposite, above
Seven pre-war United Kingdom brewery mats dating from 1935 to 1939.

Opposite, below
Some of the 1978 Bass Bill Stickers mats. On the top row are two older mats showing the first appearance of the character.

dropped and mats carried only the name Courage.

Many breweries have this kind of history, since their number has shrunk astronomically. In 1920 each town probably had a couple of independent breweries and the total number for the country was 2,900: by 1930 this total had fallen to 1,400 and by 1940 it was 840: by 1950 it was 750 and by 1960, 360. In 1970 it was 176 and in 1977 it had fallen to 105. It was at this time that David took a poke at Goliath, mainly due the effect of CAMRA (the Campaign for Real Ale) which had by now firmly captured the public's imagination. A number of fresh breweries, though small in capacity, started opening all over the country, with the result that the current figure has risen to 120. Incidentally, while it has no direct bearings on beer mats which were introduced over 20 years later, there were approximately 34,000 breweries in the United Kingdom in 1870. This reversion to traditional beer has revived nostalgia generally so that a number of breweries are now proud to recall their history and do not try to hide former takeovers as was once the case.

Bass Worthington Ltd. issued a series of beer mats featuring the adventures in 1928 of Bill Stickers, an advertising character depicted with

a suit and bowler hat and carrying a paste bucket, posters and a ladder, and this set promptly won the 1978 BBCS Mat of the Year award. The giant Watney, Mann & Truman Holdings Ltd., which

A group of early mats advertising cigarettes, including three of the pre-war Imperial Tobacco Company mats.

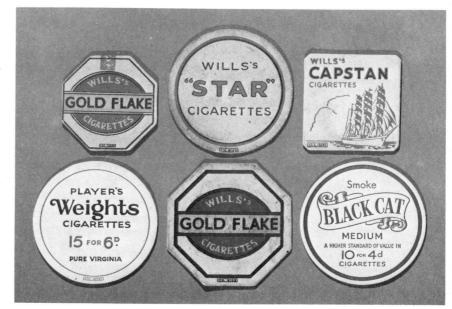

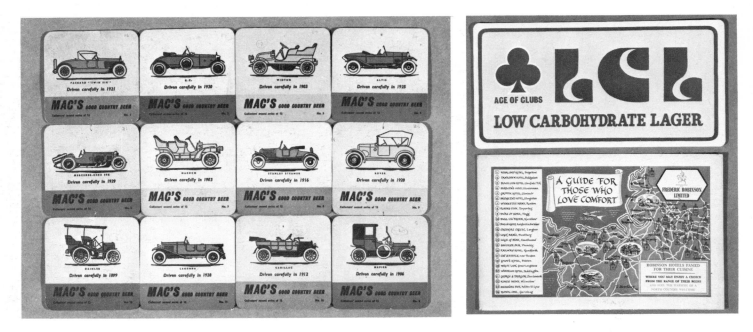

Above
McMullen & Sons' second set of cars, issued in 1959.

Above, right
Two giant mats, one from NCF (above) and one issued by Robinsons (below) in 1964.

was itself originally made up of Watney, Combe, Reid & Company Ltd. and Mann, Crossman & Paulin Ltd. which amalgamated to form Watney Mann Ltd. in 1958 and which was joined by Truman, Hanbury, and Buxton & Company Ltd. in 1971 to form the present company, has taken to resurrecting its regional image in favour of its national one, and has issued regional mats as a result. Bass Charrington have re-introduced Hancocks (which it took over in 1968) with an accompanying mat and Whitbread have done likewise on mats and pubs alike with Wethereds, previously taken over by Strongs in 1949 but

continuing to advertise jointly until Whitbreads took over in 1970.

It is interesting to note the number of breweries whose mats have slogans telling a part of this story of takeovers and mergers: 'Whitbread Trophy brewed by Duttons', 'Toby brewed by Fernvale', 'Hewitts Toby', 'Toby Ales Offilers', 'Trophy Best Bitter brewed by Tennants' are but a few. I wonder if perhaps these old breweries will also one day come back into the public eye.

Beer mats range in size from the Whiteways mat, 57 mm (2.2 in) square, to the Robinsons giant, 280 mm by 430 mm (11 in by 17 in), and there

Postcard mats. Above two versions of the Hope and Anchor Brewery mat featuring Castletown, Isle of Man, with different 'Js': this was one of a series of twelve resorts and eight boats issued in 1961. Below, the 1978 series of six postcards issued by Whitbreads.

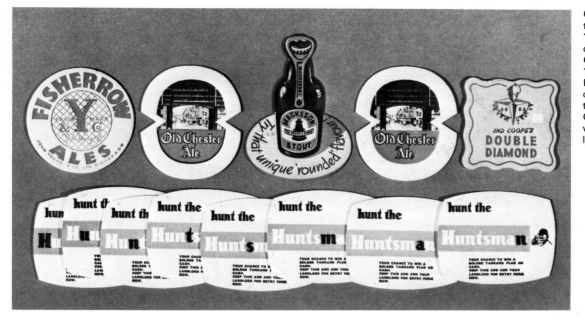

appears to be no limit to the variety of shapes which the printers can produce. Any mats larger than about 136 mm (5⅜ in) by 171 mm (6¾ in) are referred to as 'giant'. Giant mats are used on the bar as bar mats, and also in trays (hence the shape of a lot of the giants) and in fact the NCF (Northern Clubs Federation Brewery Ltd.) mats are used as a substitute for bar towels. Some of the NCF giants are a specially cut version from a whole printed sheet of single mats.

While the most common material for mats is wood pulp, they have also been printed on foam (Home Brewery and Hancocks), on cork (Ansells and Bass), on rubber (Cobbold and Magees), on glossy cards (McMullens and Guinness), on linoleum, (Ely and Wells) – not to mention pliadek, a rubberized muslin coated with flock (Mansfield and Hull), as well as plastic, perspex, wood, felt, paper, linen, leather, flock-coated card and tissue paper. Tissue paper and very thin mats are normally called cocktail mats or flimsies. Giant mats are made from wood pulp, rubber, foam felt and more recently a felt-coated foam (which seems to be the balance of the best of the previous two).

To trace the entire history of mats would be an enormous task, so I have limited myself to a few

The 1961 Double Diamond series of 20 mats (the Simonds mat is missing).

Five of the six Carrolls Irish open set and four Israeli airline mats. The two circular mats bear the marks put on by a European waiter.

of the notable events in the United Kingdom.

In 1945 Charringtons issued a set of six mats depicting leisure pursuits, for example cricket, running, bathing, which is now very difficult to acquire. McMullens issued two sets of 12 cars, the first in 1957 and the second in 1959. Then followed two sets of travel (12 mats in 1962 and 12 in 1963), and two of good country inns, 12 mats in 1965 and 48 mats in 1968 (12 designs in four colours) and then their set of carriages (48 mats), country crafts (12 mats) and then locomotives (48 mats). As can be seen methods of transport alone having provided so much inspiration, it will be some time before McMullens runs out of ideas.

In 1961 Ind Coope issued a series featuring 20 Double Diamond houses where the lower portion of the mat carried the name of the houses in which the mats were distributed and the beer available. The brewery names shown were not all companies owned by or about to be taken over by Ind Coope since they included such concerns as Whitbread.

In 1965 Eldridge Pope issued a set of mats to support their golden tankard competition. The set of mats comprised eight mats all with the word 'Huntsman' on them, each having one letter blacked out. The background was blue, yellow or green and thus there were 24 mats in the series.

Higsons issued a set of mats in 1966 which when placed together spelt out 'Higsons'. Their slogan was 'goes down smoothly' and all the mats showed a musical note, each note being progressively lower than the last one in the series. Also in 1966, Starkey, Knight & Ford Ltd. issued a series of five mats depicting scenes of interest in Devon and Somerset.

In 1968 the year after their takeover by Whitbread, Threlfalls issued four jigsaw-shaped mats which can be pieced together to form a giant beer mat advertising their blue can (a seven-pint party can).

A few Brauerei Feldschlösschen mats, together with postcard mats in four languages from 'The White Horse' at Ostend.

A selection of mats made from the more unusual materials: flock coating, pliadek, rubber, plastic, encapsulated paper, brushed aluminium, plastic-coated card, felt-backed card, cork, linoleum and perspex.

Mats have been issued by a number of food companies which when placed together form a photograph of their alleged producer.

In Ireland in 1970 Worthington issued a set of six mats which when placed in a 'w' shape spelt out the word 'Worthington'.

Beer mats are quite often used for purposes other than those for which they were intended. In Europe it is common for the waiter to put a mark on your beer mat each time he brings you a round of drinks; when you leave he cancels the mark out and starts somewhere else for the next customer. If you don't pay him promptly he leaves a mark on you!

In some Latin American countries you are given a mat with each drink and thus when you leave, it is easy for the waiter to tot up your bill.

How many times have you seen a folded mat under the wobbly leg of a table or holding open a door? Too many to say, but did you know that during the 1970 Irish bank strike beer mats were used as cheques?

Beer mats are quite often designed to be used as postcards and have been issued by many firms including Whitbread in 1978 and the Hope and Anchor Brewery in 1961; in Belgium 'The White Horse', Ostende kindly filled in the message for you. But it is only fair to say that any single-sided mat, provided it is properly drawn up and stamped, will usually get to its destination.

Printed for the occasion

Mats have been printed for all kinds of special occasions over the years, and their use is unlimited. A postcard mat has been issued advertising Cyril Smith and the Liberal Party, with a choice of replies you could tick before returning it. Both choices started 'I/We/am/are not drunk', a good opening gambit with plenty of choices for the drunk and drunker alike. Mats have also been issued by the Labour and Conservative Parties as well as by a number of other political organizations.

The postcard mat issued by the 'Sun in Splendour' pub in the Portobello Road, London records its 1967 Pub of the Year award, and talking about postcards, White Horse Distilleries Ltd. issued a set of 34 mats for all the pubs in Stratford-on-Avon in 1964, to commemorate William Shakespeare's birth in 1564.

A number of recruiting mats have been issued by the British Army inviting you to 'join the Royal Artillery', 'fly out to Singapore with the Gordon Highlanders' and to 'serve the Queen as a Queen's own Highlander'. The RAF issued a triangular-shaped mat to commemorate its 1978 Diamond Jubilee in a similar style to its set of 48 mats depicting the RAF insignia.

Royal events are always a favourite for commemorative mats. The 1977 Queen's Silver Jubilee brought forth a whole host of mats from brewers, pubs, hotels and many companies. Most of these mats were valid for a year, but the mat issued for the International Sporting Club Silver Jubilee Ball dated 7.7.77 had a life-span of only one evening. Mats of this nature are only produced in very small quantities, from a few hundred to a few thousand, as opposed to the larger breweries' requirements of millions, and thus tend to become collectors' items very quickly.

A number of breweries issued mats in 1953 for the coronation of Queen Elizabeth II including Magee Marshall, Barclays (as it then was) and Trumans. It is quite common on this type of mat for the brewery to remind you of its own age: thus the Trumans mat had the silhouetted heads of 14 monarchs and the inscription 'through fourteen reigns'. Mats were also issued at this time by such firms as Gaymers, Babycham and Britvic. The Festival of Britain in 1951 brought forth a spate of mats from such companies as Holes, Ind Coope and Taylor Walker.

Mats are often issued by the various safety organizations, especially around Christmas time when 'safety on the road' and 'drinking and driving don't mix' are popular themes.

Mats were issued by the 'Sunday opening council for Wales and Monmouthshire', campaigning for wet Sundays in the dry counties, and informed the drinking population 'eich pleidlais a benderynna' (your vote will decide).

Taylor Walker is among the few English breweries to issue mats commemorating the Olympic games in 1936 and 1948. On the other hand, the British Empire and Commonwealth games has been a favourite, with mats being issued in 1958 by Guinness, Babycham, and Coates Cider among others.

In 1964 the Munich breweries combined to issue a joint mat specifically for sale to collectors, and all the proceeds were donated to the Skopje earthquake fund.

Brewers often issue mats to mark their own

From top to bottom: the humorous Ultraproct mats, a few of the Merrydown road signs, three mats from the RAF badges set, the Myers bed centenary mats and a selection of mats advertising EMI films.

celebrations. The Stroud Brewery issued a mat in 1960 to mark their bicentenary, and Theakstons issued one in 1977 to mark their hundred and fiftieth anniversary (this incidentally was the time when they upset the labologists by producing a bottled commemorative beer with a fired-on label). Courage issued a paper star-shaped mat to support their Star Brewery bicentennial ale of 1977, which was rather an odd thing to do since the Star Brewery was taken over by Courage Barclay & Simonds in 1965 and ceased brewing soon after.

Three non-brewery coronation mats from 1953 (top row) and a selection of brewery tandem mats. On the bottom row, both sides of a Babycham mat advertising the 1958 British Empire and Commonwealth Games are shown.

Four of the five Starkey, Knight & Ford views issued in 1966, along with Hardy Crown Brewery's first mat from 1955 and two mats commemorating Stroud Brewery's two hundredth and Theakston's one hundred and fiftieth anniversaries respectively.

69

Right
The first mats from Scarsdale Brewery (1955), John Fowler & Company (1956), McLeman & Urquhart (1955), Matthews & Company (1955), Nicholsons & Sons (1950), Northampton Brewery Company (1952) and Phipps Northampton Brewery (1957). Other mats illustrated include three overprints and three special issues.

Opposite, above
A small selection of Stella Artois mats from Belgium: four commemorative mats above, eight of the Rubens 1977 four hundredth anniversary mats in the centre, and four wildlife mats below.

Opposite, below left
Both versions of the Devenish Brewery bitter mat along with their special issue for CAMRA. Also shown is the Robinson series of advertising mats.

Opposite, below right
The Courage 1951 series and a few of the 'Sammy Belles Bistrotechque' mats. The others are thin card mats—the 1956 Wrekin mat and a record request for the Cheekee Pete's disco—flimsies, and a couple of postcard mats.

Below
The original and bicentenary star mats along with some 1977 Silver Jubilee mats, the Smiths Crisps little blue bag series, and a mat advertising an Ind Coope Steak Bar in East Anglia.

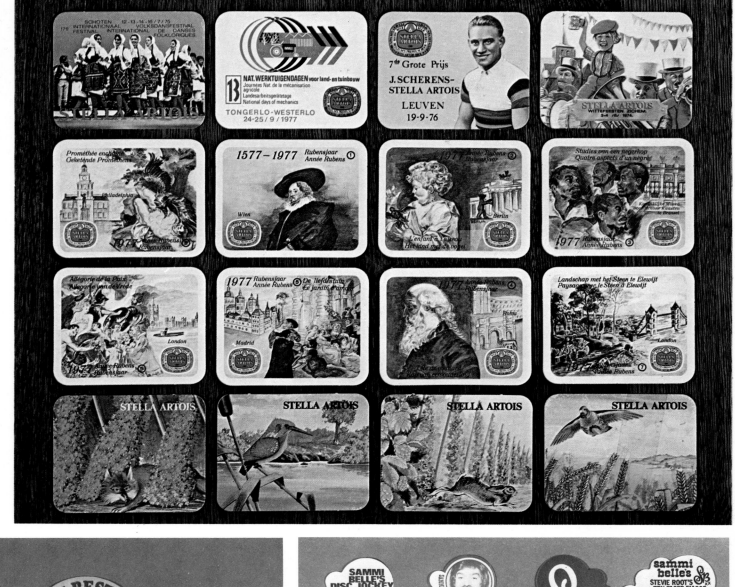

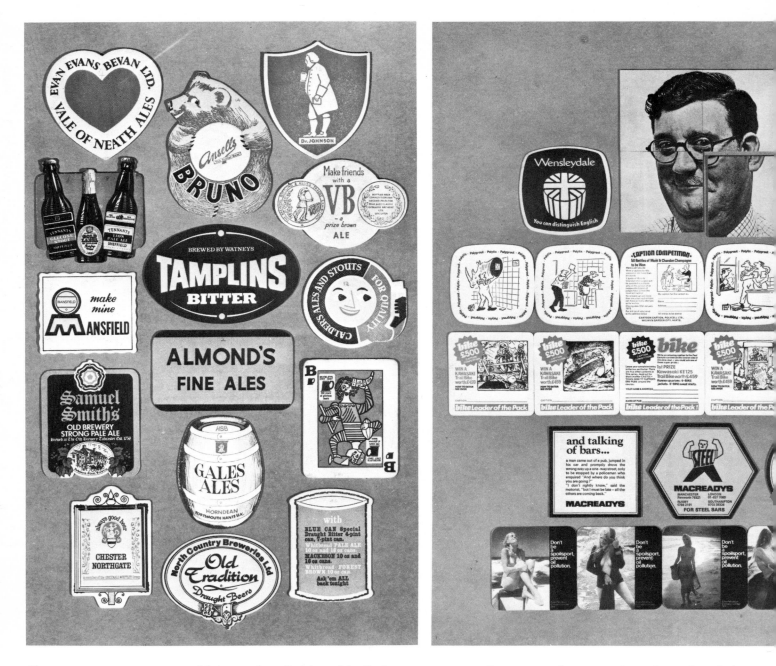

Above

Mats of different shapes. Included are a shield-shaped Barclay Perkins mat, with a figure of Dr Johnson as a trade mark, and one of the Greenall Whitley inn signs with a Chester Northgate (the issuing brewery) front.

Centre

A set of four mats which when placed together form a photograph of the owner, together with series from Polycell, Bike magazine, Macreadys and Esso (bottom row).

Mats are also often issued by the brewers soon after one of their beers has won an award. An example of this is the Guernsey Brewery Company mat of 1954, with the slogan 'first prize Olympia'. Also in 1954, John J. Hunt issued a mat with the inscription 'first prize brewers exhibition'. (Olympia, Kensington, London, is the home of the Brewer's Exhibition: the two brewers were in fact in different classes in the same exhibition, Guernsey being commended for a draught bitter and Hunts for a stout.) A shaped mat was issued by Everards in 1960 showing their brewers' awards.

A set of mats was issued by the British satirical paper *Private Eye* with a sketch of a holidaying Harold Wilson saying 'I'm alright Jack' on one side and a series of thoughts of Mr 'you know who' on the other. Needless to say the thoughts were all extracts from political promises subsequently broken: for example, 'Whatever happens we will never devalue the pound', only weeks before the pound was devalued.

Commemorative mats have been issued in Britain for such occasions as the traction engine rally at Skegness, Lincolnshire, in 1960, the Shrewsbury musical and floral fête in 1961, the gauge and tool and power press exhibition at Olympia, London in 1962, the Newark and Nottingham agricultural show in 1964, and the engineers' ball in 1964.

It is now a quite frequent occurrence for a brewery to issue a mat with its normal advertising on one side and something completely different on the other. Thus a relatively common Carling mat sometimes advertises the employment agency Pertemps, or the Birmingham Museum and Art Gallery. Similarly, Oldham brewery mats can be found with a home safety message on the reverse, and a current series of mats from Robinsons, which all have a common front, have advertisements on the back for Burger panatella cigars, the Crich Tramway museum, the Dinting railway centre, and Clean-X, not to mention the brewery's own beers. Devenish Brewery issued a

mat wishing CAMRA well at their 1978 beer festival. The Myers bed company issued a series of four mats in 1976 to celebrate their first centenary and the reverse of these common-fronted mats gave a potted history of Myers' first 100 years and notable contemporary events. A Newcastle club, the 'Sammi Belles Bistrotechque' took to issuing drip mats in 1976 which not only told you what was on for the current week, but also gave you a price reduction at the door. Mats have also been issued designed so that you can name a record request and hand it to the disc jockey, for example Ind Coope/Skol and Cheeki Pete's disco. Polycell issued a set of cartoons in 1973 for a slogan competition which they were running and in 1978 EMI issued a series of mats advertising films that they were releasing, including 'Cutter and Bone', and 'Sweeney Two'.

A cheaper method of issuing a commemorative mat is to 'overprint' (in a colour that will stand out) a normal issue mat. There are many examples of this, not the least being the ones issued by

breweries to advertise the BBCS national meetings, for example at the fifth national meeting in Walsall in 1965, overprinted mats were supplied by Ind Coope (who printed on the back of a single-sided mat), Shepherds Neame, and Tomson & Wotton. Incidentally, before their takeover by Whitbread in 1968, Tomson & Wotton claimed to be Britain's oldest brewery, having been established in 1634.

All sorts of other events have been advertised on mats, for example the 1959, 1960 and 1963 London School of Economics commemoration balls (on Fremlin mats) and the 1970 West Midlands Rag (on a Trumans mat). Scottish and Newcastle Breweries Ltd. have a large number of mats advertising the Edinburgh University students' charities, all being Younger's mats of the normal single-sided variety. A word of warning before you rush out to have your own mats overprinted: all mats are subject to copyright and before you do anything to them you must obtain the brewery's permission.

An assortment of 'special occasion' and commemorative mats. Included are both sides of a Swissair puzzle mat, the English and Welsh 'Sunday opening' mats, both sides of a Private Eye Harold Wilson mat and a couple of postcard mats, one advertising the 'Sun in Splendour' public house and the other Cyril Smith and the Liberal Party.

Noticeable collectables

Opposite
British brewery mats for use in Belgium, mainly printed in French and Flemish, and including a Whitbread set featuring characters from the British TV programme 'The Forsyte Saga'.

A major attraction to all collectors are sets and series, since there are few things more satisfying than the completion of a set. A set of mats is usually either numbered or else a collection of mats which when assembled form a word, phrase, story or picture. A series on the other hand is a number of mats each of which is complete in itself and yet with a common recurring theme or design.

One reason why people collect is because they have come across something unusual, interesting, attractive or informative and decide to keep it. It is when one has become interested in collecting that one begins to appreciate the subtleties and differences. For example, a number of mats have been issued with a blank space and small instruc-

tion: 'moisten here'. The mats of the Independence Brewery, Umu Ahia, Nigeria, advertising Golden Guinea, ask 'Who buys the next round?'. When moistened the message which reads either 'not your round' if you are lucky or 'next round on you' if you are unlucky is clearly visible. A similar type of mat was issued by the Randalls Brewery Ltd. of Jersey advertising Boxer Ales.

One of the largest series of mats in existence is the series of cartoons issued by the Binding Brewery of West Germany which runs to over 300 mats. The largest United Kingdom series is the Mackeson set of 12 Punch cartoons issued with black, white, green, purple, red and orange fronts, thus making a total of 72. This figure has

A mere 24 of the Binding Brauerei (Frankfurt) series of over 300 cartoons.

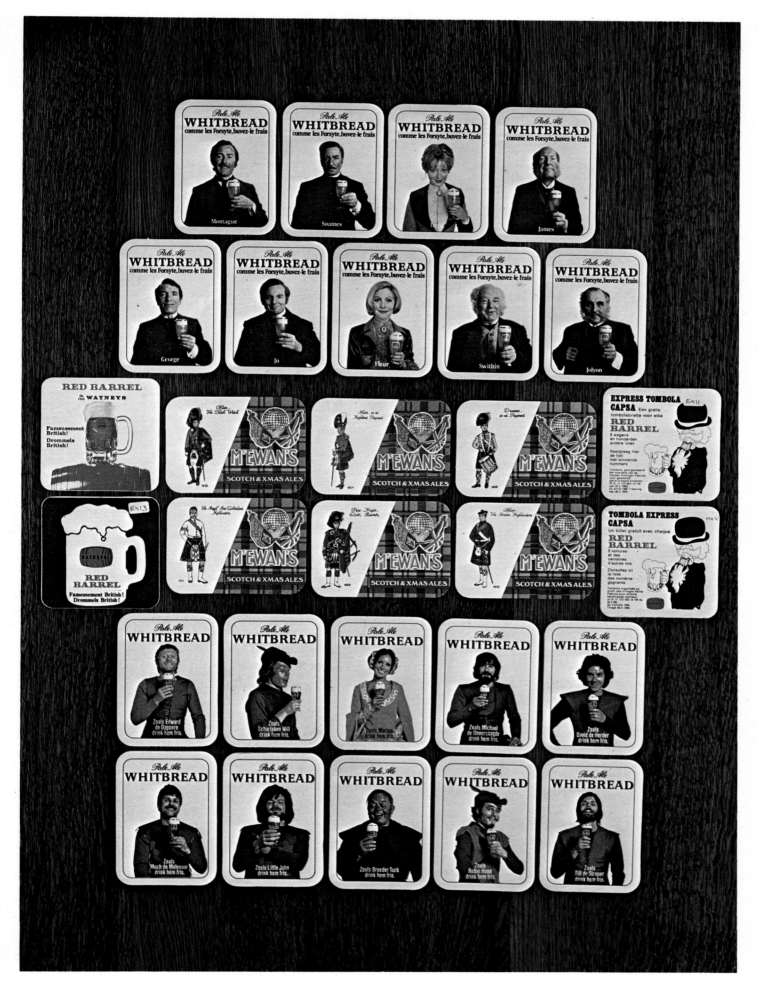

Two of the dreaded Moorfield's mats, surrounded by the shaped Skol series (on top) and the set of six Becks (Bremen) drinking vessels.

Moorfield's Ales' with the word Moorfield's being on a coloured band. The printers were allowed a reasonably free hand and so the mats were released with two different size stars, two different types of apostrophe (squarish and round), and with any two out of 34 colours printed on each mat. Yes, yes I know, you mathematicians have already cried: 2,244 possible combinations. Well so far only 112 have been recorded of the possible colour combinations of 561, the star and apostrophe differences not really being classified as separate mats.

In 1961 Courage, Barclay & Simonds Ltd. issued two sets of unusual British pastimes, such as trout tickling and cheese rolling. One set was printed in red and the other in blue. However at some time yellow must have been considered since a number of yellow proof mats have come to light. Proof mats are used by the printers as samples to show their customers. Once the proofs have been vetted and accepted, a proper production run can take place.

Proof mats tend to be single-sided although older proof mats quite often had one brewery's mat on one side and another brewery's on the other. (This was simply an economy by the printer and had no other significance.) The Allied Brewery Ltd. subsidiaries Tetleys, Ansells and Ind Coope had proof mats prepared advertising 'Brown Peter' and 'Light Peter' but unfortunately the mats were never formally produced.

In 1962 Marston, Thompson & Evershed Ltd. issued a set of six mats depicting winning race

been exceeded by Greenall Whitley who have issued a range of cartoons in a whole series of combinations which come to a total of 144 different mats to date.

From 1957 to its closure in 1970, the Wigan Brewers, Moorfields, England, decided to give the masochistic mat collector something to get his teeth into. The mats issued were of a standard design consisting of a star and the slogan 'Wigan

horses, and for some unknown reason the third, '1952 Tulyar', can be found with either a black or a red inscription. (Perhaps the printer hadn't paid for the ink, get it? in the black or in the red, oh never mind.)

And talking about credit, which we weren't, in 1965 Marstons issued mats advertising their pedigree beer in instalments: two mats bore the inscription 'you'll need the other half': one had 'pedi' and the other 'gree' on it. Rumour has it that this was a marketing ploy by a glass manufacturer to get the public to use twice as many glasses.

In 1973, Whitbread issued a series of six mats depicting 'Stanley in trouble'. Stanley gets shut in stalled submarines and aeroplanes, and on one of these mats, where Stanley is about to be killed by a shark, the common front can be found with or without a dash between the words 'now' and 'entry'.

The thin red line came back into the public eye in 1974 when Tennents issued a series of 23 mats depicting the players and manager of the Scottish football squad. The mats showed a photograph of the player and his autograph on one side and details about him on the other. Imagine the consternation among collectors when the series was apparently reissued with a thin red line which had not been there before. Subsequent investigation revealed that these mats were in fact from the first series that had been quickly scooped up by Scottish football fans; when a reissue was made, the red line was omitted. Tennents issued

another football series in 1978 depicting the Scottish World Cup squad on 26 mats.

In 1976 Ind Coope issued their first collectors' series of 15 mats entitled 'Ind Coope's Story of Beer' which were part of the advertising campaign to launch Burton ale. The mats were numbered one to fifteen and an extra number one mat was specially printed as an invitation for people to Burton ale sampling sessions which were arranged at various times and venues. The number nine mat seemed to arrive in the pubs well after the others in the set and this was thought at the time to be due to a problem at the printers. Later on a different story filtered through. A number nine mat had been printed with the wording 'cask and keg beers' and the declaration that 'keg beer had less character than cask beer'. Since Ind Coope produced the largest selling keg beer in the country and the slogan was only an opinion, the mat was not formally released and was withdrawn. A modified mat headed 'draught beers' was eventually issued which stated that 'cask beer and keg beer co-existed each enjoying its own popularity'. This set of mats won the 1976 BBCS Mat of the Year award. In 1977 the second collectors' series was issued and this set promptly won the 1977 BBCS Mat of the Year award (not due to the magnificent number fifteen mat, I hasten to add).

The vanishing hotel is a clever trick that few magicians can perform, although Tetleys managed it. Their very attractive wayfarer's mat which carried the names and locations of four of

Opposite
Higson's 'goes down smoothly' series; and on the bottom row, the Shepherd Neames's giant rubber mat, together with four of the six Ansell's/Ind Coope/Tetley 'Brown Peter' and 'Light Peter' proof mats.

The Marston's 'pedi-gree' pair of mats, together with W.T. Rothwell's first mat from 1959, a 1976 version of the Newton & Ridley (of British Granada Television 'Coronation Street' fame) mat and others.

77

Above, the Tetley's wayfarer's mat with and without 'the Wharfedale': below the correct and incorrect Whitbread mat depicting the adventures of Stanley (the dash is missing on the right-hand mat).

The 'Artic Lite' bulbs, with the 'join up the dots' game (both losers mats are shown).

was the penalty . . . I mean prize. If you were lucky or unlucky depending on your viewpoint, your dots spelt 'you're unlucky'. When first printed these 'losers' mats had a back to front 'Y' in 'unlucky', but by quickly transposing two numbers, the 'Y' became the correct way round. No need for a mirror after all. Now there's an idea for mats, the writing printed back to front so that it can only be read when held up to a mirror, and if it's written in Cockney rhyming slang, and printed in Arabic . . . but I can get carried away . . .

If you ever come across a beer mat advertising Newton & Ridley's best bitter, don't try asking for it in the pubs. It refers to the fictitious ales sold in the 'Rovers Return' pub from the British Granada Television programme 'Coronation Street'.

Finally, a word about trade marks. When the newly amalgamated Watney, Combe & Reid Ltd. were trying to tidy up their respective trade marks of a stag, a malt rake and a griffin in 1933, a national competition was organized with a first prize of £500 to find a common new trade mark. Out of the 26,000 entries, a Mr Ranklin won the prize for his simple entry of a red barrel and since that day, the red barrel has appeared on millions of copies of hundreds of different designs. Probably the other commonest trade mark on mats is the Bass triangle which was widely used as a shipping mark before 1855 when it became the mark on the pale ale label.

their houses was reissued with only three houses and a couple of red splodges. What happened to the Wharfedale hotel, we ask outselves? Mats are quite often printed in one colour and then quickly reissued in a different, more effective one, for example the Whitbread amber mat (where the printing was almost illegible in black), and the Ind Coope oval mat where a much stronger and brighter green was used the second time round.

In 1978 Allied Breweries had a bright idea: beer mats in the shape of light bulbs, with a 'join up the dots' game on one side. If your dots spelt 'you're a winner', a free half pint of Arctic Lite

Trade marks surprisingly enough sometimes move with the company, for example when Ind Coope & Company Ltd. merged with Samuel Allsopp & Sons Ltd. in 1934, Allsopps carried on using their trade mark 'a red hand' into the early 1960s. 'Ind Coope & Allsopp Ltd.' appeared on most mats issued from 1934 to 1950 when the 'Allsopp' seems to have been dropped, but the red hand appeared with just 'Ind Coopes'. (Ind Coope & Company Ltd's original trade mark of a fortress-like building was phased out completely on the merger.)

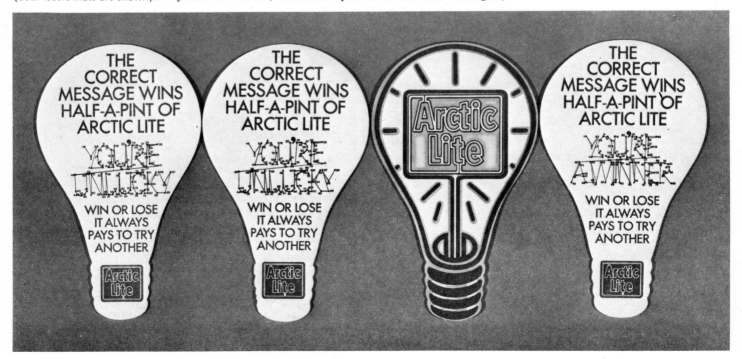

Sets and series from the United Kingdom: the Irish Worthington set, the Courage unusual British pastimes series, two of the Charrington leisure mats and two from the first McMullen & Sons series of cars.

Both sizes of the Watney's 'Fined Bitter' mat, the number fifteen mat from the second Ind Coope collectors' series and both versions of the controversial number nine mat from the first series.

The international scene

This is the area where the collector can really go to town, since the total mat issuing potential of the world is enormous. It is unfortunate that usually due to lack of space many people tend to end up collecting only mats or coasters from their homeland and eventually perhaps just brewery issues.

Most countries have issued mats from time to time: Australia, New Zealand, Canada, Denmark, Finland, Norway, France, Belgium, Holland, East and West Germany, Austria, Switzerland, Czechoslovakia, Poland, Spain and Italy have all produced a good quantity. Yet the United Kingdom leads the world in using the drip mat as a means of advertising for all types of products.

The United States is a vast country but at present its production of mats is comparatively low, partly because although there are over 100 breweries scattered through 31 states, more than 30 of them are owned by the same six companies. Anheuser-Busch owns nine, Carling three, Falstaff six, Miller three, Pabst four, and Schlitz six.

Mats from the United States, Canada and New Zealand.

A number of other companies own two each. Added to this is the fact that certain states, such as California, Indiana, Kentucky, Michigan, Ohio, Oregon, Utah and Virginia, have laws prohibiting the brewers from distributing advertising material that may have a secondary value such as coasters, as mats are called in the United States. (In some cases mats can be found which have been issued before the prohibitive legislation was introduced.)

Despite all this gloom, an original idea came from the West End Brewing Company of Utica,

Above, left
A group of African mats. The octagonal one was issued by the Kenya Police Force.

Above
The series from the Bennett Brewery of St John's Newfoundland.

Two of the cartoons from Herkules can be found among a display of Bruges scenic mats from S.A. Grandes Brasseries Réunies Aigle-Belgica. Both series can be found with two and three common backs respectively, which are also shown.

New York, which in 1961 printed coasters that were perforated onto the sides of their cardboard six-pack containers. The mats could be torn out like postage stamps and featured West End's dressed-up steins (that is, beer mugs painted to look like cartoon characters).

Canada has similar prohibitive legislation in almost all its provinces, a notable exception being Newfoundland where the Bennett brewery of St. John's issued a series of six mats depicting episodes from the history of the brewery and of Newfoundland. There are 50 breweries in the nine provinces of Canada and of these ten are owned by Carling O'Keefe, twelve by Labatts and nine by Molsons. Carlings mats are well known in the United Kingdom and may be found wherever the company has a plant, from Hawaii to Eire. Interestingly enough, although not allowed to print advertising mats in Canada, Labatts have issued a number of mats supporting their exports to the United States.

Australia, like the United Kingdom, is becoming more aware of the potential of mats as a means of advertising. Mats from all sources are now appearing: they have been issued for Karloff vodka, Capstan Kings cigarettes, Quantas airlines, and to promote wines, brands of whisky and many other things. The 18 breweries are spread all over the country but have undergone over the years the same whittling down process as those in the United Kingdom. Millers of New South Wales, for example, was taken over by the Sidney brewers Tooheys in 1967 (possibly to withstand the threat of Courage who at this time were attempting to establish a foothold in Australia). Courage have recently sold their Australian company to Tooth & Co. of Sydney, New South Wales.

New Zealand seems to be following Australia's example and is now issuing mats advertising

Mats from three series: from top to bottom, the Australian Millers Brewery; Capstan Kings (with Andy Capp) and Karloff Vodka.

Some of the Australian Quantas mats illustrating the airline's various destinations, along with a couple of older European mats (top row), a Celtia mat from Tunisia and the Albani mat (shaped like the island of Fyen) from Denmark.

paint, records, hotels, whisky, not to mention the beers of the 18 breweries. Unfortunately of these the majority are either Lion Breweries Ltd. or Dominion Breweries Ltd., and thus the mat issuing potential is limited.

Africa has produced a reasonable number of mats coming from breweries in Kenya, Ghana, Uganda, the Peoples' Republic of the Congo and Zaire, the Sudan, Libya, Tunisia, Nigeria, South Africa and Namibia to name but a few countries. Mats have also been issued by the Kenya police force and few other concerns unconnected with breweries.

Mats have been produced by the National Brewery in Venezuela, the Keo Brewery in Cyprus and the Eastern Brewery in Iraq, and by breweries in Jamaica, Trinidad, Panama, Israel, Jordan and Barbados. The Barbados brewery is the Bank's Barbados Breweries Ltd. (not to be confused with English Banks's beers of the Wolverhampton and Dudley Breweries Ltd.).

Mats are not a popular means of advertising in Asia, although they have been issued in various countries, particularly in Japan, where the five breweries and many whisky distilleries produce them. It is therefore difficult to acquire many mats

from this part of the world unless . . . wait for it . . . you have a yen for this kind of thing.

Advertisements for alcohol are not permitted in Sweden but, as in the United States, the breweries have produced mats for their export beers.

An interesting aspect of international trade is the necessity of advertising outside one's own country. This is why, for example, Whitbread issued a series of nine mats depicting the characters of the British television series 'The Forsyte Saga' printed in French and Flemish for use in Belgium. Whitbread also issued a series of ten Robin Hood characters (again in French and Flemish for use in Belgium). Watneys have also issued mats for this market as have John Smiths, Bass Charrington and Ind Coope among others.

One of the most striking and colourful series of all time is generally accepted as being the six mats depicting characters from classical drama issued by the Japanese Datsun car company, printed in English and distributed in the United Kingdom.

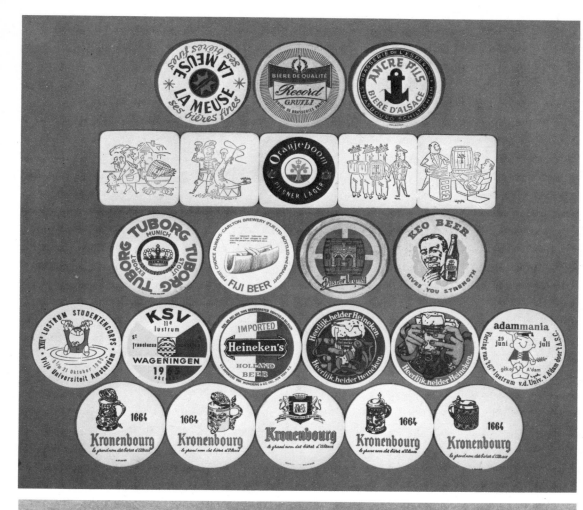

Left
Among this display are mats depicting drinking vessels from Kronenbourg, cartoon mats from Oranjeboom, special issue mats from Heineken, and a Keo beer mat from Cyprus.

Opposite, above
A small selection of mats from Europe and Asia including commemorative mats for Expo 58 in Brussels and for the 1964 Tokyo Olympic Games.

Opposite, below
Export mats from John Smiths of Tadcaster, for use in Belgium, printed in both Flemish and French.

A number of the Brasserie Artois S.A. commemorative mats, including three that recall Expo 58 in Brussels. Other export mats include a couple from the Dortmund Hansa and Union breweries.

Above
South Pacific mats from
Australia, New Zealand and
Papua New Guinea.

Opposite
Mats from Belgium, Germany,
Israel, Switzerland and Japan.
The Swiss mat tells you to
put your finger through the
mat to complete the elephant,
and those from Japan are a
very colourful set issued in
the United Kingdom by the
Japanese Datsun car
company featuring Japanese
actors.

The Swiss brewery of Haldengut issued a mat with a drawing of an elephant on one side and a hole in the middle of the mat. When one's finger was inserted through the hole, a live elephant (well, a waggling trunk anyway) was the result!

It is fair to say that everything that has been said about British mats – relating to history, sets and series, commemorative mats and general usage – is also true of mats from other countries. Perhaps the only real exception to this is that the widest range of mat advertisers can be found in the United Kingdom (with Australia the closest runner-up, although a long way behind). The following ratios will give some idea of current comparative mat production in different parts of the world. For every one mat issued in the United States or Canada, there are five mats issued in Australia and New Zealand, 100 in the United Kingdom and 1,000 in Europe.

Lamots, Carlsberg, Tuborg, Löwenbräu, Holsten, Becks, Heineken, Oranjeboom and other breweries have all issued numerous mats, and space does not permit a full description of all of them. But it would be criminal negligence to omit the most prolific and consistently colourful mat producer in the world, the Belgian Brasserie Artois S.A. (Stella Artois as it appears on their mats). Stella Artois has issued sets and series covering such topics as early aircraft, early sailing ships, events from the Olympic games, folklore, towns, cities, wild life, works of Rubens and even a series to commemorate Expo 58 in Brussels. So attractive are their mats that collectors who have specialized in certain fields often include Artois as an exceptional additional category.

Practical collecting

Most collectors of mats do not consciously go out with the intention of starting collecting. A number of wives and girl-friends maintain that it is a disease that is contracted and should be cured if possible. However it does not discriminate against the sexes as it can attack males and females alike.

Certainly collecting of any kind is a bug which is usually passed on by an incurable collector who makes you wonder not so much why you don't collect yourself but why you hadn't started years ago. The first couple of mats are usually quite harmless but the the time 20 to 30 are acquired the rot has set in. This is the time where collectors take the plunge and with a devil may care attitude announce to the world, 'I collect beer mats, do your worst'. It is now that friends, relatives, work-mates, neighbours and even casual ac-

quaintances get pestered, 'Oh if you get a chance to pick up any beer mats from such and such for me it would be very much appreciated'.

Acquiring mats from friends in this way is the best way for youngsters to start and definitely the cheapest, but for the enthusiast who likes a pint there has never been a better excuse to the wife than, 'I haven't got the latest mats issued by so-and-so brewery so I'll just pop in and have a quick one'. As you can imagine wives do get suspicious when after five or six similar visits and with the pockets bulging you slur, 'just one more for the set dear'.

Exchanging mats with fellow collectors is a very satisfying method of expanding a collection since older collectors generally like to encourage youngsters and this means that someone else is trying to find the mats you want as well as yourself. It is very easy if the mats are exchanged face to face and both parties can see exactly what they are getting, but when trading through the post, be careful to make sure that the condition of the mats is accurately described. Apart from mats which can be described as 'mint' (perfectly clean) or beer stained the following defects should be specified: pin-holes, sellotape marks, air stains, fold marks, breaking-up edges, writing on mats, varnish, woodworm holes and generally dirty. These defects should be listed for both sides of the mats and not just for the 'sunny side'.

Generally speaking mats are exchanged on a one for one trading basis on the assumption that they are of a similar type, age, condition and rarity. Obviously due allowance should be made for inequalities to balance the trade.

While it is convenient to mark the mats you have in your collection and also the duplicates which you may wish to trade, your methods may not coincide with the collectors with whom you do business. It is recommended therefore that mats be lightly marked with a soft pencil which can easily be erased. Sticky labels are not recommended since subsequent removal can damage the mat surface permanently.

The joining of a mat collectors or similar collecting society is a real must for the serious collector. Most societies tend to formalize the hobby and although this gives great benefits to the members, it does not always appeal to the casual collector.

Most societies organize meetings for collectors to get together and exchange mats, views and general observations, and this is the only sure

way to keep in touch. Similarly most societies issue a magazine or newsletter and this keeps you abreast with the latest releases.

When collecting mats from pubs, it is worth remembering that someone has taken the time and trouble to put the mats on the bars and tables to brighten up the decor and protect the surfaces, and it is only common courtesy to request the landlord to give you the mats that you require. Always providing he has time, he will usually give you clean mats of all the different types he has available.

Writing to the companies that use mats as an advertising media is a comparatively effective way of expanding a collection, but once again courtesy should be the watchword. Requests should be polite, not too demanding and accompanied by a stamped addressed envelope of a suitable size. A number of the British breweries have an arrangement with the BBCS whereby all requests for mats are dealt with by the society. This relieves the brewery of an irksome task, ensures that collectors get clean and current mats and helps the society to enroll new members.

So far only free or comparatively inexpensive methods of acquiring mats have been discussed but the time may come when you have so many mats that they only way to obtain new ones is to either bid for them at an auction (auctions take place at all BBCS meetings and are run through the post in 'The Beer Mat Magazine', the journal of the BBCS) or to buy them from a retiring collector. Purchasing mats in this way can be effective but also very costly.

Once a number of mats have been collected the question must be asked, where shall I put them? On this subject a few distraught wives and incidentally a few vociferous husbands would not be lost for a reply.

Storage does become a very real problem as one's collection grows, and since the only fully satisfactory method is expensive, I shall lead up to it gradually.

Adorning walls with mats is a popular method with college students but produces air stains on the mats with either pin holes or sellotape marks and is therefore not recommended. Similarly hanging mats up with string or cotton or on tape strips, while decorative at the outset, only produces disfigured mats.

Mats can be stacked or piled on shelves, but without some form of protective covering they will rapidly become very dusty and the top mat of each pile air stained. They can also be placed between polythene sheets and kept in large books in a book case. This can be an ideal method for storing a part of a collection, for example delicate mats such as foam mats or flimsy (cocktail) mats, or particularly rare mats which you wish to show but not have handled. But it is bulky for the collection as a whole, and is only practible for small or specialized collections or for people living in large houses.

Another storage method requiring considerable space is the use of display cases or showcards, which if not glass fronted and encased should be covered in polythene. It is here that the amateur photographer has an ideal solution since photo-

One of the mats from the
1978 Tennents footballers
series (both sides) along
with a number of the subtle
differences that can be found
on mats.

graphs of mats are easy to carry and display and
occupy less space.

The recommended method for the new collector
is cardboard boxes (such as shoe boxes or cut
down apple boxes) that enable the mats to be
stood up on end. By dividing up the boxes a
number of rows of mats can be stored. If the mats
are not packed in too tightly there will be room
for head cards to mark further sub-divisions.
While cardboard boxes are the best method
mentioned so far the very best is the use of a chest
of drawers. A wooden drawer of 69 cm (27 in) by
30 cm (12 in) by 15 cm (6 in) will house approximately 1,000 mats and thus a five-drawer chest
will house 5,000 mats, assuming a maximum mat
size of 10 cm (4 in) by 10 cm (4 in).

Wooden chests of drawers with subdivisions
are the tidiest and most effective way of protecting
and housing large collections, although giant
mats require a drawer to themselves, since they
will need to be laid flat. Any mats larger than the
standard size of approximately 10 cm by 10 cm
(4 in by 4 in) should be housed along with the giant
mats to ensure that the maximum number of
standard-size mats are kept in other drawers.

Having dealt with ways of acquiring a collection and housing it, a couple of interesting
observations can be made. The first is that most
serious collectors, irrespective of the size of their
collection, can remember whether or not they

have a mat in their collection just by looking at
it, doubts only arising with mats in sets or series.
And the second is simply that mats housed in
wooden chests of drawers and generally kept tidy
seems to attract less adverse observations from
wives; the principle, out of sight, out of mind, is
definitely valid and the cost of the cabinets is
probably a small price to pay for a tranquil home.

A method of sorting out a collection will
obviously be required and there are many different ideas on this. My personal method is as
follows. Brewery issues are divided from non-
brewery ones, the former being sorted in alpha-
betical order of British breweries and chronologically within breweries. Current and obsolete
breweries are all kept together. Other British
mats are sub-divided as follows: soft drinks, ciders,
wines, liqueurs, spirits, hotels, pubs, restaurants,
army, navy, Air Force, air lines, travel and car-
hire, crisps, other foods, cigarettes and tobaccos,
safety, newspapers, car sales, garages, drip mat
printers, fêtes and festivals, theatres and panto-
mimes, rags, bottlers and finally a large miscel-
laneous group. Within each of these major
categories further divisions are made according
to issuing company and within these smaller
divisions the mats are either kept chronologically
or by brand name whichever is the most appropriate. The same basic divisions are also used for
mats from other countries. Another method of

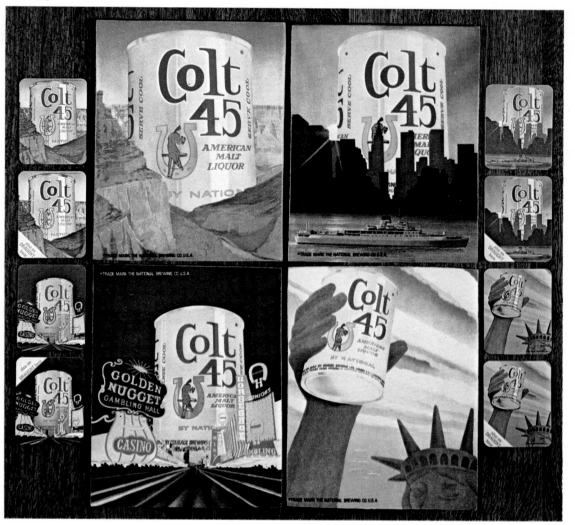

Felt-coated foam 'Colt 45' giant mats with their wood pulp counterparts.

sorting brewery mats on the continent is to keep them in order of towns with breweries as sub-divisions. Whatever method you choose if you can find the relevant sections the goal has been achieved. It is essential to have some kind of filing system to prevent duplication and to quickly establish whether or not you have a mat.

From time to time you will acquire dirty mats which should be cleaned. Great care must be taken with all cleaning methods and the following are recommended. For wood pulp mats gentle rubbing with fresh moist bread will help to draw out the stains as will the careful application of a soft artist's rubber (the type that can be kneaded in the fingers). Felt mats can be rinsed in luke warm soapy water and dried by pressing flat between two towels. Most modern foam mats can be washed in the same way but the older type (which tend to be single coloured and rather ordinary in design) can only be soaked in cold soapy water and then very gently dried as above. Thin card mats may be cleaned as wood pulp mats but the flimsy tissue mats and those made of pliadek are best left completely alone. Rubber mats may be lightly scrubbed in warm soapy water and dried as before.

The best way of protecting a new or recently cleaned mat is by storing it in a self-seal air tight polythene bag which is then kept in a dark place such as a chest of drawers. Where the mat itself is not of wood pulp or any other reasonably strong material a piece of cardboard should also be placed in the bag to help keep the mat straight. Lacquering a mat causes the board to go a yellow colour and makes it look worse after a time. Mats should be kept dry since the board tends to warp if damp; particular care must be taken with used mats as these can sometimes grow mould.

Mats should be kept out of sunlight and cigarette smoke and if they are ever out on display a form of protective covering is essential.

Since we started this chapter by discussing bugs it seems appropriate that we should end on the same note, and this means woodworm. Since most mats are made of wood derivatives they make an ideal home and food supply for this particular beetle. Always carefully inspect mats which have been stored in lofts before adding them to your own collection lest you move in the bug. Unfortunately the worm seems to prefer the older mats and being a generous little fellow he eats a bit out of each mat as he passes through rather than polishing them off one by one.

Collecting mats is a hobby which can require very little effort on the part of the collector. It can be inexpensive, and yet enjoyable, entertaining and enlightening. It appeals to both sexes, to all age groups (the BBCS has members ranging from nine to 90), and from all walks of life—it really has got 'something for everyone'.

APPENDIX

SOME USEFUL ADDRESSES
FOR LABEL COLLECTING

Labologists Society of England

Keith Osborne
211 Pinewood Park
Cove
Farnborough
Hampshire

Victorian Beer Label Collectors Society

Rod Gillard
8 Bunting Court
Lalor 3075
Victoria
Australia

The Adelaide Labology Group

Jim Hepworth
5 Willow Crescent
Cambelltown 5074
South Australia

Unser Steckenpferd

Winfried Friedel
Postfach 30 04 05
D-7000 Stuttgart 30
West Germany

East Coast Breweriana Association

Leon Beebe
14 Manor Drive
Rt 3
Mount Airy
Maryland 21771 USA

FOR BEER MAT COLLECTING

British Beer Mat Collectors Society

Brian Pipe
28 Northumberland Road
Harrow
Middlesex
HA2 7RD

South Hurstville R.S.L. Coaster Collectors Club

Jack Murphy
South Hurstville R.S.L.
   Club Ltd
Connells Point Road
South Hurstville
New South Wales
2221 Australia

Gambrinus Club de Belgique

Michel David
Rue de la Croix 33
1050 Bruxelles
Belgium

B.D.M. (Bierdeckel-Magazin)

Reinfried Stark
Grasamer Weg 3
8501 Cadolzburg
West Germany

I.B.V. (Internationaler Brauereisouvenir–Sammler–Verband)

Winfried Friedel
Postfach 30 04 05
D-7000 Stuttgart 30
West Germany

ABBREVIATIONS USED ON BEER MATS GIVING AN INDICATION OF THEIR COUNTRY OF ORIGIN

This list will prove helpful for foreign mats, which can prove a headache to the mono-lingual collector, as can mats issued for export (although fewer mats are issued for export than for the home market, a notable exception being the English John Smith's brewery of Tadcaster).

(The dashes indicate the name of a brewery.)

Word or words on mat	Most likely country of origin
ÖL	Sweden
–Bryggeri AB	Sweden
–Bryggerier AB	Sweden
A/S–Bryggeri*	Denmark
A/S–Bryggeriet	Denmark
A/S–Bryggerier	Denmark
A/S–Bryggeriene	Denmark
ØL	Norway
A/S–Bryggeri	Norway
A/S–Ølbrggeri	Norway
OY–or–OY	Finland

Pivovary	Czechoslovakia
Pivo	Czechoslovakia
Piwo	Poland
Browar	Poland
Cerveja S.A.R.L.	Portugal
Cervezas S.A.	Spain
Biirou	Japan
ΖΡΘΟΣ	Greece
–S.A.	Greece
ПИВО	Russia
Sor	Hungary
Bira Fabrikasi	Turkey
Biyar	India
Birra	Italy
–S.p.A.	Italy
V.E.B.	East Germany (post 1945)
Brauerei AG or K.G. or GmbH	Germany
Brau	Germany
Brau	Austria
–Aktiengesellschaft	Austria

Bier	Holland
Brouwerij–N.V.	Holland
Brasserie S.A.*	Switzerland
Brauerei A.G.	Switzerland
Pivoara	Yugoslavia
C.A. Cervecera	Venezuela
Cerveceria – C.A.	Venezuela or Mexico
Brasserie–Et Cie	Luxembourg
Brasserie–S.A.	France
Bière	France

Note: In some cases, the above information will not help give an indication of the country of origin; Switzerland, for example, has three languages in use—French, German and Italian. If the issuing brewery can be identified by reference to a brewery manual, this can give an indication of a mat's origin. The printer's name, if shown on the mat, can also help.

*A/S, S.A. is the equivalent of 'Ltd.'

ABBREVIATIONS USED WHEN DESCRIBING BEER MATS

Mat itself

SS	–Smooth surface
PS	–Pitted (embossed) surface
REV	–Reverse
OBV	–Obverse (front)
S-SDD or 1/0	–A single-sided mat
SBS or 1/1	–The same design on both sides of a mat
1/2	–A different design on each side of a mat

Details concerning brewers and printers

B.N.	–Brewer's name
B.N.A.	–Brewer's name and address
B.I.	–Brewer's initials
P.N.	–Printer's name
I.N.A.	–Importer's name and address
T.M.	–Trade mark
B & B	–Brewed and bottled by (not to be confused with bed & breakfast!)

Shape

Sq.	–Square
Hex.	–Hexagonal
Circ.	–Circular
Oct.	–Octagonal
Rect.	–Rectangular
Tri.	–Triangular
Ov.	–Oval
Shd.	–Shaped (usually accompanied by a description)
Rnd. Sqr. or Quartic	–A generally square mat with curved sides
Rnd. Tri. or Circulateral	–A generally triangular mat with curved sides

Colours (normally abbreviated to two or three letters)

Red	–RD
Blue	–BLU
Green	–GN
White	–WT
Yellow	–YW
Orange	–OR
Indigo	–IND
Violet	–VLT
Black	–BK etc.

ACKNOWLEDGEMENTS

Very special thanks go to Ness, my beloved wife who erased my errors by typing my manuscript, has been a constant help, and above all, turns a blind eye to 25,000 beer mats. Thanks are also due to Solly Teff for his help and advice, and to Peter Gilardi for the loan of some mats to help with the illustrations.

I would like to place on record my personal and sincere thanks to all the breweries and printers who have helped the BBCS and myself over the years, and without whom tegestology wouldn't have been born. Apologies are made in advance for any attempts at wit contained herein.

Brian

I should like to thank Joan Connew and Peter Dawson for the loan of labels for illustrations, for providing inspiration for the manuscript and for their invaluable advice. I am grateful to Dave Pratt and Michael Bishop who also lent some of their labels but above all, my sincere thanks extend to my wife, Beverley, and my family, without whose patience and devotion half of this book would not have been possible.

Keith

All the photographs in this book were specially taken for the Hamlyn Group by John Webb.

The author and publishers would like to thank Bass Charrington and Company for permission to reproduce from their archives the 1843 East India Pale Ale label on page 16, and the labels from the album of infringements and forgeries on page 18.

INDEX